D1329459

FEARLESS
AND
fabulous

FINDING YOUR WAY
THROUGH CHANGE AND BEYOND

A COMPILATION BY
Cathy L. Davis

FEARLESS AND FABULOUS
Finding Your Way Through Change and Beyond
UpsiDaisy Press

Published by **UpsiDaisy Press**, St. Louis, MO
Copyright ©2020 Cathy L. Davis
All rights reserved.

No part of this publication may be reproduced, stored in a retrieval system, or transmitted in any form or by any means, electronic, mechanical, photocopying, recording, scanning, or otherwise, except as permitted under Section 107 or 108 of the 1976 United States Copyright Act, without the prior written permission of the Publisher. Requests to the Publisher for permission should be addressed to Office@daviscreative.com, please put **Fearless and Fabulous** in the subject line.

Limit of Liability/Disclaimer of Warranty: While the publisher and author have used their best efforts in preparing this book, they make no representations or warranties with respect to the accuracy or completeness of the contents of this book and specifically disclaim any implied warranties of merchantability or fitness for a particular purpose. No warranty may be created or extended by sales representatives or written sales materials. The advice and strategies contained herein may not be suitable for your situation. You should consult with a professional where appropriate. Neither the publisher nor author shall be liable for any loss of profit or any other commercial damages, including but not limited to special, incidental, consequential, or other damages.

All contributing authors to this anthology have submitted their chapters to an editing process, and have accepted the recommendations of the editors at their own discretion. All authors have approved their chapters prior to publication.

Cover and Interior design: Davis Creative, DavisCreative.com

Compilation by Cathy Davis

Fearless and Fabulous: Finding Your Way Through Change and Beyond

ISBN: 978-1-7347971-0-7 (paperback)
       978-1-7347971-1-4 (ebook)

2020

JUST BECAUSE I NEVER

by Lori A. Henson

When I wondered if a change
Would end in failure,
I trusted my instincts
And trusted myself.

Just because I never,
Didn't mean I would falter.

When circumstances
Threw me a curve,
As I grasped at many prayers,
I held my head high.

Just because I never,
My dreams weren't going to die.

Now I'm lit from within,
Living a life of new passion.
It's okay to be grateful,
Looking forward renewed.

Just because I never,
Didn't mean I never could.

Table of Contents

What Do You Want, Butterfly?

"Now is the time to understand more, so that we may fear less."
— Marie Curie

Change is inevitable. How we react to it is purely our choice.

We find ourselves in week six of self-quarantine. The 2020 global virus pandemic has roared in, overtaking an otherwise beautiful Spring. Our state has implemented "Shelter in Place" status, with only the life-essential brick-and-mortar businesses allowed to stay open. Restaurants have completely closed with only a select few remaining open for curbside pick-up. Those of us who can, are working from home with "highly-suggested" limited access to essentials—grocery stores, pharmacies, medical care, etc. We can still walk the dog in our neighborhoods (local parks are closed) but are asked to keep at least a six-foot distance from each other and wear masks in public.

It's an amazing time to be living on Earth…and even that phrase, "on Earth," seems so new—so awkward—and does not easily land on this page. We've entered a new millennium—what many are calling a "New Earth." The virus which threatens to destroy each of us individually has also found a way to unite the entire planet as medical teams across the globe are working together to find an antidote, a vaccine, a cure—any way to reduce the loss of life and gain control over the virus.

What an AWESOME time to be fearless and have LESS FEAR! Everything we know as "normal" is changing. When we make it to the other side of all this chaos, there will be new ways of living, new ways of doing business, and new ways of interacting with family, friends, and neighbors.

CHAOS + COURAGE = CHANGE

The cocoon we've been living in will no longer be needed. How we emerge from this isolation will be entirely up to us. It will be our job to burst forth and create the life we want. A new world is ours for the making.

So, I ask you, "What do you want?" What do you want YOUR new world to look like? It's one thing to be able to navigate change and make necessary pivots in real time, but what if we think BIGGER? What if we decide right-here, right-now, what we want our new world to look like?

Many of us never ask ourselves what we want. Perhaps it's because we think we have enough already...or don't deserve it...or maybe we figure it's too late, anyway—what difference will it make? But if we don't ask ourselves what we want, there is no way to know if our dreams are even possible or if we have the courage to make them come true. If we are unable to ask ourselves what we want, we turn to our tribe—our family, our colleagues—our friends who "get us" at our core.

Our power lies within and among.

Much like a single butterfly, each of the seventeen contributing authors has decided at some point in their life to make the personal choice to break through whatever is holding them back, reach for the light, and create a life worth living. Each has found the courage to go for what they want and make the changes necessary— not just in order to survive, but to thrive.

Each year, during Fall migration, Monarch butterflies join together for their northward journey. The strength of the group—also known as a kaleidoscope — serves to protect and support each other along the way. Similarly, the power of the collective shines forth in the stories shared between the covers of this book. United in collaboration, these authors share their wisdom as their gift to you on your personal journey.

Please accept our invitation to join our kaleidoscope as we fearlessly navigate, hand-in-hand, towards a fabulous new earth!

"What do you want, Butterfly?"

Let's go do that.

As a professional brand and author consultant, **Cathy Davis** founded Davis Creative, LLC in January of 2004 after a career in marketing high-net-worth financial services. Over the past 15 years, their client base has grown to include all 50 states and several foreign countries. Known for developing creative brand messaging, Cathy and her team of veteran marketing professionals began introducing clients to self-publishing in 2005 as a means to build brands, change lives, and transform thought leaders into well-known experts.

Books, printing, and publishing have always been an integral part of Cathy's life—from making books as a student in college, to working for a printer and a major book retailer after college, to collecting books for her personal library. A former board member of the St. Louis Publisher's Association, she lives in metro St. Louis, MO with her husband, Jack, and Canine Office Cheerleader, Chewy.

Cathy L. Davis
cathy@DavisCreative.com
www.DavisCreative.com
www.facebook.com/DavisCreativeLLC/
www.facebook.com/creativewritingcafe
www.linkedin.com/in/cathyldavis/

Doing What Scares You

If you had told me when I was in law school in the late 80s that I would one day be running my own business, leading a law firm of multiple attorneys, and having the level of success and satisfaction in my career that I have been able to achieve, I would not have believed you.

I never remember wanting to do anything other than practice law. From the age of 4 or 5, I wanted to go to law school; it was always the answer I gave when a relative or friend would ask me what I wanted to be when I grew up. And as I grew up, it morphed into a solid reality. I had a sense of wanting to correct injustices. I remember, first, seeing and experiencing the differences between how men and women were treated—and then this expanded to realizing the differences between how people were treated based on their skin color, where they were from, how they talked, how much money they made, and more.

At a very young age, I became painfully aware of a situation of horrific domestic abuse in a family I was close to. It was a family that, from the outside, seemed put together, kind, and loving. This idea that domestic abuse was something foreign, something that happened to other people but not to the people I knew and loved, came crashing down.

I went to law school hoping to learn how to do some small part to correct the injustices I had seen in the world and to help victims of domestic abuse. Family law was a natural path for me and I have been grateful to spend the majority of my career pursuing the passion I had as a child.

At the end of every year, I hold an office meeting. I tell my employees the story of how I started this firm. Some have heard it many times by now, but no matter how many times they've heard it, they humor me and listen—sometimes filling in the details before I can—as I remember a path that was scary and exhilarating and that led me here.

I explain how I overcame a fear that, frankly, should have been larger than it was. I was younger when I started my firm and still had that feeling of immortality, of being invincible. Looking back, if I had to make the same decisions today, I'm not sure I would. I didn't know enough to even know everything that could go wrong. I was fearless in a naive way, but it gave me the courage to go out on my own, not knowing if I would succeed, and for that I will always be grateful.

A business I knew had asked me to do their legal work if I went out on my own. It wouldn't be nearly enough to provide full time work, but it was a start. At the time, I was in a job I liked, but which was unfulfilling and not challenging. I went home and thought about their offer and realized I wanted to be challenged every day. So, I resigned my then-job, took my young daughter out of school for a month-long road trip, and took out a $3,500 line of credit (you could start a business for much less those days!).

That entire first year of having my own firm, I was scared to even tell my parents. I was worried they would be afraid of how I would support myself and my daughter. I was worried they would be right. I look back on that first year and it was scary—terrifying at times—but it was also fun. It was a huge challenge. It was new. I had to build up a clientele, take care of my daughter, and I didn't know if it would work. It actually ended up being a great year financially because I was so worried I wouldn't make it, that I saved almost everything I made. I learned that fear can sometimes be a good thing and you can save a lot of money when you're scared about when or if your next client will walk through the door.

It would be easy to look back now and say I succeeded because I wasn't afraid, because I dove headfirst into every issue, and had an undying will to prevail. And while I hope some of that is true, the real truth is that I spent a lot of time being scared. It wasn't the best feeling in the world, but it pushed me to succeed. It pushed me to work harder, be more aggressive, and prove I could do this. This is a book about being "fearless and fabulous," so maybe I shouldn't admit this, but I don't think I'm fearless, and I think that's actually a good thing.

That first year was hard. My daughter was young and at that age where it felt like she was constantly sick. I would bring her to the office with me and she would sleep on my two office chairs pushed together. I brought work home—this was before the years of laptops. I would bring my daughter into the office after school and on vacation days. As soon as she could read, she would help me organize the office and do filing (yes, she is wonderful at alphabetizing, she learned very young!).

At the end of the first year, I was shocked to look back and see I had built up a clientele, I was getting referrals, and I might actually be able to make this work long-term. I got over my fear and actually looked at my bank account! I studied it, checked it because I thought it must be inaccurate, and realized I had been successful.

While I spent much of that first year in my office, working from home, and building my firm, I would be remiss to make it seem like I did this alone. While this was my firm and I was and am so proud of that, I could not have done it without the support and help of friends. At the end of my first year, I went out to celebrate with a good friend who had been extremely helpful: picking up my daughter from school, listening to me worry I wouldn't make it, and reassuring me I would. To this day, I don't know what I would do without the support of good friends. I've learned that true friends are the ones who believe in you even when you can't.

There have been many changes since I opened my firm. I've seen the attorney advertising market go from an ad in the yellow pages to social media, online ads, websites, and more. Part of me is afraid I am going to miss that next development, that the market will change and I'll be left out. That fear of when the next client will walk in the door has never left me. But I think fear can be good and it has pushed me many times to stay on top of technological changes, work harder, and take on more challenging cases so I can keep growing and learning.

My parents instilled a great work ethic in me, but I've found that a little fear to keep you going, keep you on your toes, can be a good thing.

Other people in my office sometimes give me a hard time because I still talk about how I'm afraid of maintaining this business. I care about my employees and their lives. I care about being able to pay salaries and continue to build this business for myself and my employees, who have become like family. While my business is now much more stable than that first year, when I had more reason to fear I wouldn't make it, that a client would not walk in that door, that first year has stayed with me. That fear of not making it has pushed me, and even though we think of fear as a bad thing, I also think fear has pushed me to better places.

Advertising and social media are something I was resistant to at first. I thought it was tacky, it was new—I had to get used to social media. It can be scary to dive into something you don't understand. I've made myself learn it (as well as I can), and now I can have fun with it. This thing I was once terrified of and didn't understand is now something I embrace. Not only does it help with business, but I like connecting with the community.

One of the things I find the most gratifying about my business is that I have been able to develop strong relationships with clients, colleagues, and local businesses over the years. There is a great sense of trust in my community. I still operate with one of my biggest clients on a handshake deal we made nearly 30 years ago. It's inspiring to me that we can still do that. As an attorney, I would probably advise clients not to do that, but the trust I have with this client is more important to me.

In thirty years, I have been fortunate to work with numerous employees who have become like part of my family. You're not going to find that with everyone, but these relationships are worth it and are one of the most treasured parts of my work.

Fear puts pressure on you. I've found I am someone who performs well under pressure. Thinking on my feet, pinch hitting, making things work when my back is against the wall.

This business has grown. About ten years ago it took off. I went from just me and a paralegal to now having numerous attorneys, support staff, and locations. We've had some growing pains. A larger business has brought different challenges and different stresses. I've had to change some of the ways I had been doing things for years and to put even more trust in the people with whom I work every day. Sometimes I miss those days of just me and one paralegal. But I wouldn't go back. I wouldn't change it.

As my business has grown, one of my goals has been to provide my employees with the same thing I was able to gain in my firm—the opportunity to have a career they can be proud of, meaningful work, and the ability to have time with their families. To have their career and not sacrifice family and time with children. This is one of the reasons why so many of my employees have become like family. I have tried hard to create a work environment where everyone acts and is treated like a professional. While it may not always seem to make the best business sense or financial sense on the surface, it has remained important to me to make sure my employees don't have to sacrifice their personal lives for their professional lives.

While I may look back and wish I hadn't worried so much, I know that worry is part of that good kind of fear, and that it can lead to good things. Even if I was frustrated and worried, the love I have for my business, my clients, my employees, and the results I've been able to achieve are better than anything I could have imagined.

We all want to be fearless and fabulous. To be invincible, to make it out of sheer determination. But I can't pretend that's my story. My story is of being fearful at times, of using that fear and having it drive me to better places. I don't think you need to be afraid of fear, you just need to know you can overcome it. Fear has made my life fabulous and I couldn't be more grateful.

Continued...

Barbara has been practicing law in the St. Louis Metro East area for over 30 years. She concentrates her practice in domestic litigation, real estate law, and general civil practice.

Barb received both her Bachelor of Arts and Juris Doctorate from Washington University in St. Louis, Missouri. After receiving her law degree, Barb was a stay-at-home parent for a year, returning to the legal field in 1989 as a law clerk to the Honorable Kent Karohl on the Missouri Court of Appeals, Eastern District. After completing her judicial clerkship, Barb worked as an associate at a law firm in Edwardsville, Illinois, followed by an appointment to the Madison County State's Attorney Office as lead attorney in both the Child Support Enforcement and Anti-Domestic Violence Divisions.

Barb opened her own practice in Edwardsville, Illinois in April, 1993, with a focus on family law, including appellate work and complex relocation cases. Today, she is proud to offer legal services not only for family law, but also criminal defense, real estate, general civil litigation, and probate work. Barb has expanded the firm and services offered in order to address the full scope of her clients' needs.

ShererLaw.com
www.facebook.com/shererlaw/
www.twitter.com/BarbaraLSherer
www.linkedin.com/in/barb-sherer
www.youtube.com/channel/UC6w-LrMxi7tDk31qpqhBDPw

CHRISTINE MELTON

Making Something Out of Nothing

It's my mother's fault. She filled my heart with inventive motivation when she said, "Don't just sit there, young lady. DO something!" I could see the vacuum and dust rag awaiting me. At ten years old, what in the world could I do that would be enough to ward off mother's chores? As the saying goes, "Necessity is the mother of invention". I was desperate. I needed a job. So, my creativity went into high gear. I became a motivated self-starter.

I found cereal boxes and masking tape. Armed with those two "starters", some scraps of fabric, ribbon and a button, my unique box purses were born. I sold those cute little things to a local gift store. A young entrepreneur was born!

My mother also instilled in me the belief that I could do anything I put my mind to. And I tried a lot of things. I had so many projects going she would often ask if I ever finished them. Some ideas were discarded or left undone. The point was that I tried and kept trying until something worked.

Curiosity played a big role in my creativity. I once made a raincoat out of the Famous Barr's department store shopping bags. I thought the bags were stunning with their big orange, yellow and blue mums. Of course, the bags had "FAMOUS BARR" written all over them. I didn't care. It was the opportunity to make something out of nothing that spurred my welling creativity. I still have that raincoat. Can't get my right arm in it, but it's with me as a reminder to think outside the box.

Making something out of nothing really has been my life's theme.

I never want to look back on my life and say "I wish I'd..." Yes, I'm a risk-taker to the core. I've had many days riddled with fear of my next move, but I was never crippled. The truth is, no matter the depth of the hole you feel you are in, there is always a little light coming from above. When you finally realize all you really need to do is get up off your knees, stand up and walk out of the hole, your life will change. You'll discover you are always at choice.

I've had many opportunities to act fearless in my life. At age 24, I became an instant step-mother of three and business co-owner in a male-dominated industry. Out of the need to have marketing materials for our clients, I created brochures, flyers and newsletters on my typewriter and copy machine. After 20+ years, I left my husband and business partner. At age 44, I drew upon my experience of making something out of nothing and started my own business of graphic design.

What makes my life fearless and fabulous? It's doing what I love. I've never taken a job or a project that I didn't believe in. I've tried a lot of things. At one point I thought people were saying, "Geez, what's she up to now?" If one path hit a big roadblock, I'd make a right turn and try something else. I have never felt I HAD to keep going on something that didn't serve me. It just made me unhappy. And being happy is a high priority! That means I keep learning, growing and building upon my zest and enthusiasm for life. It can actually be quite simple to ward off the dark spirit called doubt. If it creeps up behind you, turn around and BLOW IT AWAY! Focus on the future, not the past.

Thanks to Emilie Wapnick, I got permission to be a serial creative. A *multipotentialite* is a person who has many different interests and creative pursuits in life. ... *Multipotentialites* thrive on learning, exploring, and mastering new skills. We are excellent at bringing disparate ideas together in creative ways. This makes us incredible innovators and problem solvers."

Keep a journal. In it, write what's in your mind and heart. The next day re-read yesterday's entry. Then, in today's, turn yesterday's negatives around into positive statements of what you "DO WANT" your life to look like. Example: "Had a day where everywhere I went, I took a wrong turn. Couldn't wait to get home to the safety and security of my familiar surroundings." The next day I wrote, "The confusion I felt yesterday is lifting and my confidence is growing." Write it even if you don't completely believe it. Do it anyway, because the next day you'll re-read the positive entry and it will build upon itself. This is a great way to make your life Fearless and Fabulous.

Don't let yourself get away with fear. Years ago, I accompanied my 2nd husband, Jerr, on one of his teacher workshops. At lunch the superintendent invited us to play golf at his club after the event. Jerr was SO excited but I could feel fear creeping into my psyche. At lunch, I could feel myself getting sick. I KNEW what was happening. I was a novice golfer and the terror of looking very foolish was creeping into my mind. I excused myself from the table and headed to the ladies' room. There I grabbed myself by the shoulders, spun myself around and looked into my fearful face. The conversation went something like this: "Oh no you don't young lady. You KNOW what this is about, and you are *not* going to get away with it. This is important to your wonderful husband. Now, put your big girl panties on and go have fun." My fear was "blown away," and I felt the nausea begin to subside. We ended up having a great time. I probably still golfed terribly but cared less!

Facing the fear is one thing. But more important is identifying what it is you are afraid of and making an agreement with it.

Jerr and I had not lived in rural Missouri long. Foreign country to this city girl. I'd been rooting around in a cedar closet, when I brought my head up to face the largest spider I'd ever seen. Jerr came running with his shoe to my shrieking. Instead I asked for a jar. I got the spider in the jar, tightened the lid and poked holes for air. Throughout the next day I looked it up and down; watched it move around. I stared into its many eyes. I even put it on my nightstand just to stretch my fearlessness. I NEVER want to be afraid of something I don't understand. It was amazing what I learned about it. It was just a creature far smaller than I, probably as terrified of me as I was of it and living life as a spider. No harm. After a day of that, I took it down the road two miles and released it so it couldn't find my closet again.

Fear can be a habit. We get stuck doing the same things—many that don't serve us. So, if you want to change something, switch it up. Wear your underwear backwards for a day. That'll shift the way you think! Move the furniture around. Brush your teeth with your left hand for a week. It will make you laugh!

Jerr and I had planned to build our Bed & Breakfast Retreat Center on the 30 acres in rural Missouri we had miraculously been led to. Six months after moving there doctors discovered Jerr had an aggressive cancer. After a nine-month battle, my beloved husband died in November 2002. At 52 I was alone, 100 miles from everything I'd known my whole life, and left alone with our dream that I wasn't quite sure how to make real.

"You don't always need a plan. Sometimes you just need to breathe. Trust. Let go and see what happens." – Mandy Hale, Livelifehappy.com.

And, sometimes you just need to close your eyes and jump in.

So, in March 2003 I drew upon the skill I'd mastered in creating something out of nothing and began to renovate the old trailer across the lake to become my Bears' Den Bed & Breakfast. With the help of incredible friends and family, I opened my new business eight months later. The day I took my first reservation I remember thinking "I'm really doing this!" In so many ways I learned to be fearless in a world of 'I don't know how or what to do with this' which included spiders, lizards, snakes, ticks and a multitude of weird sounds that came from the dark nights.

It was a fully loaded experience having The Bears' Den. I put a lot of "tools in my toolbelt," as my Jerr would say. The progression of my life, when viewed from above, as if a flow chart, shows the amazing trail of the evolution of my soul and my spirit. Although it has often felt like I was wandering in a desert, there was always somewhat of a path to follow. As I set my desires for more, opportunities showed up and I acted upon them—often with blind hope. And as my pattern shows, if it didn't pan out, I'd move on to the next one.

In 2009 I left the world I'd created in the country and moved back to St. Louis not having a clue what was next. I moved in with my mother (then 97). Out of sheer boredom (no grass to mow or beds to make), I enrolled in Culinary school. Then, age 60, expanding my mind with new skills was a huge boost to my passion for learning something new. This time I got to use my brains, not my brawn. There were only 9 in my class. Ages ranged from 18 to 37…and then me at 60. One morning when class let out and the halls filled with students, I heard a young woman yell from the end of the corridor, "Is it true? Are you really 60?" Not missing a beat, I yelled back, "NO. I'm 61!" No one ever called me grandma. Although one of my classmates confided that she was concerned for her grandma who was very frail. I asked her how old her grandma was. She said, "Sixty-four". Put that one into perspective! After graduation and a year of lugging heavy equipment as a Personal chef, I ditched that idea and was ready to spawn a new one. The choice of getting a job was far from my mind.

How did I start something new, again, at this age? Well, I've been known to say…"I don't know where I'm going, but I KNOW IT'S GOING TO BE GREAT!"

Drawing upon my multipotentialite experiences, it was, again, time to create something out of nothing, and Purely by Heart Designs emerged. This time with paper and glue—creating custom greeting cards. My niece, now in her 40's, told me she still has the card I had made my sister when she was born. It seems I've come full circle. Maybe my ultimate dream has always been to simply CREATE—something.

One thing I DO know is that I will never stop learning or being curious. It's part of living an inspired life. It's too much fun. And, "if it ain't fun, I ain't doin' it."

I love this quote by Bob Proctor. "Set a goal to achieve something that is so big, so exhilarating that it excites you and scares you at the same time." I believe the only failure is in denying yourself the opportunity to soar with what you love.

My mother passed away at 100. She had always said, "Honey, you just got to keep moving." And as I'm sort of a clone of my mother, I figure that's advice to be taken seriously. As Mavis Leyrer, age 83, put it: "Life's journey is not to arrive at the grave safely, in a well-preserved body, but rather to skid in sideways, totally worn out, shouting "HOLY SHIT…WHAT A RIDE."

I'm not waiting. I'm enjoying the ride NOW.

Continued…

Christine Melton is a native St. Louisan and serial-preneur. Her life looks like a flow chart of opportunities to develop businesses out of challenges needing solutions. At age 24, Christine co-founded a food brokerage firm to which she attributes the building of her many business skills to those 15 years of sales/marketing/advertising, graphic design, business management and accounting.

All of her past roles have served her well in the development of a diverse list of business enterprises, which include that of gym owner, life coach, graphic designer, wedding officiant, band singer, bed and breakfast owner, Certified Chef, and caregiver/companion.

Now, at age 68 she works with her first love—paper—and is the passionate innovator of yet another business, Purely by Heart Designs, where she creates unique 3D greeting cards.

Christine believes nothing is impossible and that following your heart's desire is what makes life worthwhile and wonderful—at any age.

purelybyheart@gmail.com
www.purelybyheartdesigns.ecwid.com
christine@purelybyheart.com
www.purelybyheartdesigns.com

DERLENE HIRTZ

My Moment of Surrender

"Choice is a powerful thing, suffering is always optional."

– Stacey O'Byrne

The first time I heard this quote, I thought to myself, "no way, I don't have a choice."

Have you ever met someone that you felt had it all together? That someone was beloved by a community; looked like she had it together; was the first called to join in and join up; was the one asked to volunteer because "no" was not a word she practiced. She laughed with you, cried with you, supported you; always with a smile on her face. Her perceived expectations: show up, suit up, and shut up. What does Oprah call it? The "need to please disease."

She was me.

I remember driving home that night, arriving to a dark, quiet house, the light, cool air wrapping around my body like a snake; I was exhausted after fifteen hours of educating children and attending night classes at college. I was feeling alone. My husband was out of town; my kids had grown and had lives of their own. The voice in my head was reminding me constantly: your son is going to Afghanistan for the first time. He was an Army soldier and the fear that he was going to march straight into harm's way had been consuming me for months. Just thinking about it created a burn deep inside my soul that I could not get to go away. When I attempted to say his name and "Afghanistan" in the same voice, I would literally choke and start crying.

Yes, I know fear. Paralyzing, life-stopping fear. Fear ruled my life. I believed I had no choice. I love my son and he was going off to war.

I had considered myself a "closet" woman of fear because I allowed fear to consume me while I was alone. Then I would go to work, social events, and the gym with a smile on my face as if I didn't have a care in the world. There were only two people who knew I was living in a constant state of anxiety and fear; they were sworn to secrecy.

Have you ever had one of those moments where it was like the "devil" stood on one shoulder and an "angel" stood on the other one? That is what I sensed when I pulled into my driveway on that night.

"Don't go into the house, you are not in a good place," the devil said, as I thought about my son heading to Afghanistan.

"You're fine, you're strong, you got this," the angel said.

I remember thinking, "what should I do? Go to my girlfriend's house and say, this little voice in my head said I shouldn't go home, so here I am?" The thought of that made me laugh as I hit the button to open the garage door.

I consider that experience the best worst day of my life. Why? My son was being placed directly into harm's way and I was paralyzed with fear. I decided to do something about it. It was my moment of surrender. That is when I held up my hands, bowed my head and asked for help.

Walking in the house, I dropped my purse, book bag, and jacket; I then stopped at the counter. Banging my hand on the counter, I had a knock-down, drag-out fight with God. I said, "I am done." I begged, pleaded, negotiated Derek's safety in return for whatever God needed from me; and after much exertion, began praying. I was finished feeling so sad, anxious, fearful and if it was time for me to "go" I was good with it. I even let God know (because we tell God, huh?) that He had my permission to make that decision. And what if God didn't make the decision? Would I?

I picked up the phone and made a life-changing phone call. It was in that phone call, I found the hope I needed. Honestly, I had to borrow hope until I could allow hope to be born within myself. It was then I realized it is true: choice is a powerful thing; suffering is always optional. I had chosen to suffer by burying myself in fear and closing out people who loved me.

From that moment on, I let go of suffering and embraced empowering choices. I have never looked back. I started chipping away at "the need to please disease" and began embracing the power of self-worth, self-love, gratefulness, and self-forgiveness.

What happens when we begin making decisions based on self-love? Shift happens! We understand we are worth the investment of time, money, and energy. We begin seeing ourselves the way the universe sees us; a ball of shining light waiting to be shared the way God (or whatever you call your Higher Power) designed us, which is to play big. Playing small does not serve us or others. Holding ourselves back because we don't want to brag about our awesome selves, believing we have to step into the shadows to give the other person a chance to shine, or fearing we will hurt someone's feelings because we state our truth; those are society-infused beliefs we have picked up along the way.

My advice: own that you are an amazing woman, understand that you are fearless because you have known fear and you are fabulous because you once knew ordinary. This empowerment is a moment of surrender; an acceptance that you are ready to learn from the past and embrace the potential within you. The greatest moment of my surrender led to my Journey of Intention (the title of my book) and this all happened when I was almost fifty years old!

This awakening of my spirit, doctors call it menopause; they tell me I am going through "the change." I say, "you bet I am!"

I began embracing my new journey and my desire to serve using my experience, education, and training. I had enjoyed teaching the many students as a school teacher; but I realized it was time to step into an entirely new chapter of life. I bought a networking franchise, TEAM Referral Network, and started my company, You Empowered Services. I am the first entrepreneur in my family and am proud of myself. As a trainer and master coach of Neuro Linguistic Programming (NLP) I help other business women get out of their own way so they can get on their way.

I have been asked why I purchased the St. Louis franchise of TEAM Referral Network. My answer: I love to network and build relationships with like-minded professionals. I get to meet amazing and talented business owners and entrepreneurs. I help them build their businesses. I have seen life-long friendships be created and support systems born entirely out of a single introduction. I am grateful for this opportunity to make a positive impact in St. Louis by helping others and supporting their dreams.

You Empowered Services grew out of my desire to serve others who have had experiences much like my own. The first time I was asked what my dreams were, I said, "What do you mean what are my dreams? I just want to get through today." That is a hopeless and scary life to choose.

As I watch clients and the attendees of my *Train Your Brain for Success* Bootcamp begin to shift their thinking to serve their dreams, my heart is full of love and happiness, I can barely hold it inside! That is my greatest definition of success.

We are fearless because we have known fear. We are fabulous because we have felt ordinary. Embrace your story, your experiences, your wisdom, and be that beacon of hope for all to see!

When I tell my clients, "get out of your way so you can get on your way," their next question is, "how do I do that?" I believe what you feed grows, what you starve dies. Neuroscience is now able to prove this. Do you know someone who is a chronic complainer? The brain has changed shape because they constantly are bathing their cells with negative thoughts! It is what leads to anxiety and depression. That is scientific!

When we listen to the voice in our head (you know the voice that just said, "you don't have a voice in your head") and allow it to remind us that we are not good enough, smart enough, thin enough, or successful enough, we are not empowered to live our best, most successful life. We call that voice the ego, ANTS (annoying negative thoughts), or the itty bitty shitty committee. When we feed the ANTS by buying into the lies, they grow until they destroy our relationships, dreams, and our true selves.

What do you invest in that allows you to believe you are "bettering" yourself? Updated phones? Computers? Wardrobe?

The most important investment is our mindset where we learn "choice is a powerful thing, suffering is always optional." We are operating on a (so to speak) DOS 2.0 system. Our decisions are based on our very early years (ages zero to seven) when patterns of behavior were learned by modeling the adults in our lives; that is, developing patterns such as how we react or respond to anger, sadness, fear, hurt, guilt. Most people never "upgrade" these behaviors. It is scary to think that decisions to marry, discipline a child, or make money are based on what we learned as children.

As we begin the process of truly investing in ourselves, we discover our power has been there all along. This power that most likely has been buried since we were children, contains a light so bright that sometimes we feel like we are on fire (no, it is not menopause). Those dreams that we have never shared with anyone for fear of being laughed at, well, they become goals. One day we wake up and we see those goals are becoming reality. That only happens when we step into our true, authentic selves. When we begin to stand in our power.

Fearless. What a word!

Fabulous. What a word!

Fearless and Fabulous—Well, that is Unstoppable!

We can now call ourselves fearless because we have overcome fear. We can now call ourselves fabulous because we recognize ordinary does not exist. Fearless and Fabulous; this is our great Moment of Surrender!

I was once told to think about the words "toxic friendship." There was a friend in my life who was just that: a toxic friend. As I thought about those two words, I began seeing a pattern. See, when toxins are introduced into our bodies, at first there may be subtle changes. Maybe we don't feel as strong as we once did, perhaps our sleep is off, or we don't have much of an appetite. As more toxins are added, they begin to comprise our lifestyles and our lives.

That is exactly what negative self-talk or chronic complaining does to our brains. Little by little we bathe our minds with the toxicity. Until one day, it is who we have become. And we find ourselves driving home from a long day of work, like I did, and saying, "I am done."

If you were ever asked to write a letter to your younger self, what advice would you give her? I used to do a workshop on this very question. My answer? "Don't change a thing." I say this because if anything would have been different in my life, anything at all, this moment right now would be different. And I am blessed, grateful, and excited to be the person who gets to remind you: *Choice is a powerful thing; suffering is always optional.*

Let this be your greatest Moment of Surrender!

Continued…

21

Derlene Hirtz is an NLP Trainer, Master Coach, author, speaker, and franchise owner of TEAM Referral Network. Through her training and coaching business, Derlene helps professional women move past the need to please mindset and create the life they dream, desire, and deserve. Derlene also offers coaching for women who seek personal growth within their spiritual development. Derlene chose to recreate herself after she celebrated her 50th birthday. She is the author of "Journey of Intention—Life Made to Order."

As a franchise owner, she creates an environment of excellence and provides face-to-face networking in order to grow businesses through relationship marketing.

Ultimately, Derlene's greatest successes are being married to her biggest supporter, Steve, for 39 years, her two children, Derek and Krista, their spouses, and greatest of all, three grandchildren with a granddaughter to be born this summer.

Derlene@youempoweredservices.com
www.youempoweredservices.com
www.teamreferralnetwork.com
www.facebook.com/derlene.hirtz
www.linkedin.com/in/derlene-nlpcoach/

Happy on Purpose

In a research paper he authored in 1996, Dr. Dan Herman coined the name for the phenomenon of the fear of missing out, more commonly referred to as FoMO. I had a severe case of it. How did I know? I am happy to tell you.

I spent years on self-discovery via the guidance of more than my fair share of life coaches, spiritual advisors, mindfulness practices, and all the self-improvement books I could get my hands on. I was aware that I could not be happy unless I was in the thick of '*it*'—It, my friend, is FoMO. I was never certain what '*it*' was, but I was always willing to give '*it*' the old college try. I was forever in search of my purpose.

You know when you bump into a random friend from school (for my friends from St. Louis, Missouri, we know that means high school)? The two of you share a little small talk then that evolves into 'what are you up to now?' That unpretentious, simple little word 'now' was always my elephant in the room. I was aware that I had become somewhat of a joke among a few of my acquaintances. I had developed the reputation of trying/beginning/making a go at _____ (this is where you can fill in blank with '*it*', a job/hobby/sport). When I realized I was not good at whatever you filled in that blank with, I would move on to the next thing, and the next in perpetuity.

I married and started a family in my early 20s. Who knew that would turn out to be my first insight as to what made me unconditionally happy? That one thing that made me completely happy: being a mom. Thanks to my husband Dino's hard work ethic and commitment to our family, I spent about 10 joyful years as a stay home momma with our two daughters, from Kindergarten to the beginning of high school. Motherhood remained the one thing that made me feel like I had found my purpose. For those years, I had found my 'it'—my career was momhood. I cheerfully (almost too much for my daughter's comfort at times) volunteered as a room mother, a lunch lady, a librarian, a Girl Scout Leader and PTO member. I took super mom status very seriously. Sadly, volunteer opportunities are few and far between at the high school level. With that realization, coupled with knowing my daughters were old enough to take care of themselves, I felt thrust once again into what would become another 20 years of searching for '*it*' again.

This time I took my time deciding what the '*it*' was; what I wanted to do when I grew up. I gave several Multi-Level Marketing (MLM) opportunities a whirl. Friends and family encouraged me, some assured me that I was a natural at sales, that I could 'sell ice to an Eskimo'. Sadly, I learned that while MLMs can be a wonderful career path, the lesson for me was that this is not the case for an extroverted introvert such as myself.

I then returned to a medical office where I had worked early on in my mommy life. I am sure you are familiar with the phrase, sometimes you just can't go back. You guessed it; it did not take long to see that that was the moral of that shortlived story for me.

The transition from the self-confident 30-something, to the worried, insecure 40-something was not anything I expected or was prepared for. As a result, I began to feel like the only way to deal with any situation was to appear on the outside the exact opposite of what I was experiencing on the inside.

I had a brief reprieve from my search for '*it*' when I took what I thought might be my dream job as a buyer and merchandiser of apparel for a Country Club Golf Shop. I loved everything about it, especially my coworkers. In the end, sadly, the environment proved to be toxic.

Society would have us believe that to be successful, you needed more, more friends, more material things, more money. Just more, more, more. That is where my downward spiral picked up speed and straight lines began to blur, making it hard to see any light at the end of the tunnel.

The ah ha moment, the catalyst that sent me reeling into the 5th dimension and thrust a new set of wheels into motion, was when I realized that only my finding sobriety would help me continue to find my way to my true purpose. I attribute my return of sanity and serenity to my recovery and a series of God moments. The biggest gift I was given as a direct result of sobriety was the renewed interest in continuing my search for '*it*' with vigor and clarity. There was one thing I knew for certain; I was as happy as I had been during my career mom days. It became obvious to me that I was going to find my purpose, by making others happy. I was embarking on the next chapter of finding out what '*it*' meant to me now.

Over the next several years I enjoyed learning new skills. I can say with 100% sincerity that all of them have contributed to the success of my current business. I dabbled in the art of Improv Comedy. I bought a beautiful guitar and took a few lessons, only to return it after I had realized I would have to cut my nails to play. I went back to school to finish my degree in social work, with my sights set on helping others in recovery. I again changed my path and attended the community college for a year learning American Sign Language (ASL), with the objective of being an interpreter for AA Meetings.

I have one younger sister, Tracy, and we are as close as twins, though we are 3 ½ years apart. Of the two of us, I lean toward the reckless side, left of center if you will, Tracy is quite the opposite, sensible and reasonable. My husband Dino, and Tracy's husband Joe, affectionately refer to us as R&L BC, the right and left butt cheeks. Together we make the perfect team.

Our conversation about opening a coffee shop together began in jest. Our husbands thought we were nuts but went along with our planning and dreaming. We put pen to paper and began our market research aka drinking copious amounts of coffee at small coffeehouses around town. When tossing around the name for our shop, we landed on two words which were tattooed on my arm two years prior, for my 50th birthday. The idea for the tattoo began with just a steaming mug of coffee, it was as simple as that. The words Espresso Yourself were added as an afterthought and an homage to my love of expressing myself through being creative and my love affair with everything coffee. You can call it fate, or kismet or a self-fulfilling prophecy, but the name Espresso Yourself Coffee & Café was born.

Through a series of fortunate events, we signed a lease for a space in the perfect neighborhood, in the perfect community, in the perfect part of town that was experiencing a resurgence of new business growth. It was as if we were chosen to be there, it was, I believe, divine intervention. We opened our doors September

2018 on the weekend of the Southampton neighborhood block party, Macklind Days, and never looked back. I am a living, breathing example of a woman who has experienced her dream materialize before her eyes. I am a proud entrepreneur.

Tracy and I decided against having separate business cards, so we came up with the idea of just having our first names on one card (we really do everything together) and our titles, Chief Happiness Junkies #1 & #2. Obviously, I am older, so I am #1. I feel the need to pinch myself almost daily when I look around at our guests enjoying one another, or getting a little work done outside the office in a space my sister and I lovingly cultivated. My nurturing momma persona has played a huge role in creating a homey, cozy space for anyone that enters to feel as though they have entered my home, not just an ordinary coffee shop.

Earlier I mentioned Improv, guitar lessons and numerous attempts at completing my higher education. I can say that each of them has contributed to my success as a small business owner. First, improv comedy is much more than being funny, you learn to think on your toes and trust your partners in the act with you. These skills have proven invaluable in dealing with my business partner as well as our amazing staff. Besides, I try daily not to take myself too seriously. I like to have fun doing what I love. Next, although I never did learn to play the guitar, we hold Open Mic Nights once a month and I have seen more than a handful of musicians put themselves out there simply for the enjoyment of it and entertainment of others. Finally, my one year of ASL has given me the ability to carry on basic conversations with a deaf guest, and that makes my heart skip a beat.

Knowing what I know now, it is only natural that the creation of the welcoming, homey atmosphere of Espresso Yourself bears a lot of similarity to the space I created at home while raising my daughters. It is in my DNA to care for people.

When you enter the shop, belly up to the counter to order. If you look just beyond the espresso machine you will see the words Good Vibes Only on the office window. I *feel* those good vibes every day when I go to work. I hear our guests say they feel them too. Coming to Espresso Yourself Coffee & Café, the home of the Happiness Junkies, is a positive experience and in my humble opinion, there is nothing more fabulous.

One of my favorite words is synchronicity. According to Wikipedia, synchronicity is a concept, first introduced by psychologist Carl Jung, which holds that events are "meaningful coincidences" if they occur with no causal relationship yet seem to be meaningfully related. I believe that synchronicity was at work during my quest for '*it*' and the ultimate discovery of my purpose.

I feel it was no accident that the perfect neighborhood for Espresso Yourself to call home, presented itself when it did. Nor I do not think it was a coincidence that I chose a coffee-related tattoo a year before I knew for certain that I would be moving forward with my dream. I also know in my heart that it was not just luck that so many of my past experiences, my time learning Improv, ASL, and guitar, have become such a large part of my reality today. It took being open to the possibilities and allowing them to unfold as they should. All that to say, I credit the synchronicities and the willingness to accept them for my success.

Since Espresso Yourself Coffee and Café opened its doors in late 2018, I have had some well-meaning friends, during casual conversation, mention they are thinking ahead to retirement and joke about my starting a business at this stage in my life. It's all I can do to nod and smile. I think about how lucky I am to have been given the gift of time and the tenacity to realize what my end game was and what I needed to be genuinely happy. I know for me, what I do is what I am meant to do right now, in this very moment in time. I am beyond a shadow of a doubt, blissfully happy, very much on purpose.

Continued…

Jules Karagiannis is co-founder and COO of Espresso Yourself Coffee & Café, a charming neighborhood coffee shop located in the Southampton neighborhood of St. Louis, Missouri. Jules manages the Marketing/Social Media Strategies, the Monthly Newsletter Communication and Event Planning of the shop.

Prior to opening Espresso Yourself Coffee & Café, Jules, her husband and daughters, owned and operated a fine dining restaurant in the Chase Park Plaza, located in the Central West End neighborhood of St. Louis.

Jules is extremely proud of her role as the wife of her hard working and talented chef husband, Dino, and mother to their beautiful grown daughters Mary and Eleni.

Her years in the hospitality and service industries had served her well when Jules and her sister Tracy made the decision to open Espresso Yourself Coffee & Café. She enjoys decorating and takes pride in her ability to make her customers feel like they have walked into their best friend's home. Jules passion is making the world a happier place.

jules@espressoyourselfcafe.com
www.espressoyourselfcafe.com
@EspressoYourselfcafeSTL
@es.presso_yourself

Comfortably Caffeinated

According to dictionary.com:

Fearless [feer-lis] adjective: without fear; bold or brave; intrepid

Fabulous [fab-yuh-luhs] adjective: exceptionally good or unusual; marvelous; superb

Not exactly two words I would have ever have used to describe myself. In fact, I've always been one who has relied on consistency, familiarity and normalcy with an overwhelming desire to just fit it. Someone in the psychology profession may say this is a result of a severe lack of stability in my early life.

I lost my mother at the young age of ten. My sister, Jules, and I were raised by our father, who tried, sometimes to a fault, to make up for this loss in spite of suffering from depression and addiction. Our home life consisted of little structure or supervision. In my early teens, I inevitably took on a role of caretaker. My post-secondary education consisted of one semester at home and one semester away and then ended as I opted to stay home to care for our ailing father. Just two weeks before my 19th birthday, I started my first full-time job as a receptionist at a chemical company. I spent more than 18 years with that company, holding various positions and climbing through the ranks.

I was the typical career mom of the 90s. I dropped my two boys off early in the morning as daycare was opening and often picked them up as they were getting ready to lock up for the evening. Working late into the night after putting the boys to bed was not an uncommon sight. I recall only one spontaneous career decision I ever made…I quit. I was 12 years into my career and well established with the company. I was the go-to person for almost any procedural question from any position. However, within less than a two-year period, my husband changed jobs, I miscarried, we moved our family to a new home, I gave birth to our third child and I lost my dearest friend of 20 years to a horrible disease. My consistent and comfortable world had been turned upside-down. These devastating events in my personal life forced me to re-evaluate my professional drivers. I no longer had the desire to climb the corporate ladder. Rather, I decided that I needed to be home and cherish time with my family. I hadn't discussed it with my husband.

I hadn't even given much thought to what I was going to do or how we would survive on just one income. I simply walked into my boss's office one morning and told him I was giving my two weeks' notice. Never in my life had I ever done something so drastic without deliberation. But I knew it was what I needed to do.

Though caught off guard, my boss accepted my resignation. Within those two weeks before leaving, he and I discussed alternative options. After an offer to continue in their employ, I agreed to stay on in a part-time role. Ironically, approximately two years later, management changed and my part-time role was eliminated. I was given two options – resign or return to a full-time position. Accepting the fact that at this point I had four children and my household depended on my financial contribution, I returned to the forty-hour work week. Though I no longer had the desire to reach executive status as I had before, I loved my job and appreciated the familiarity it provided. I remained with that company for another four years until the division I worked in was ultimately dissolved and I was laid-off.

Though uncertain of what my future held or how I would handle starting all over again, I looked forward to finally having some time off with my family while searching new career options. As fate would have it, however, prior to the end of my time with that employer, I received an offer with a competitive company. As many different roles as I had held previously, this job was one I had never done. But the offer included being able to work from home two days a week. This would afford me the balance between career and family that I had been seeking for so long.

It was not easy leaving the company that I knew so well and the people who I had grown to love. Some of whom had supported me through my father's death and celebrated my marriage and the birth of my children. They were a constant in my life that I had depended on for so long.

One short week later, I started my new job at my new company. I was terrified. I was starting over in my late thirties. In my entire adult life, I had only known one company and I knew it like the back of my hand. But I had been forced out of my comfort zone. I was suddenly put in a position where I had to meet a new set of co-workers, build new relationships and learn new processes. It helped, though, that I remained in the same industry. Many of the products, suppliers, and even customers were familiar, so that eased the transition.

Thirty years in the same industry, 27 years of marriage, 25 plus years as a mother and 20 some-odd years in the same house—heck, I don't even move my furniture around very often—I believe there is something to be said for consistency, familiarity and normalcy. So, when Jules and I started talking about opening a business together, of course I thought it sounded like fun. It certainly was fun to fantasize about, but I don't know that I truly thought it would ever become reality.

Starting something brand new in my late forties would be risky and out of my element. Jules and I talked about this "dream" of opening a coffee shop for about three or four years. We talked about it on and off so much that I'm certain our husbands stopped taking us seriously. Jules collected furniture and décor, while I spent my lunch hours driving around looking for locations. We had discussed various areas around St. Louis and narrowed our search to South City. Though we grew up and both live in the suburbs, we loved the revitalization going on in the South City areas and the migration of younger families. We looked for someplace near both neighborhoods and businesses. Together we did our due diligence by reading articles, perusing books and visiting other area coffee shops to check out and make note of what we liked and didn't like in their décor, set-up, and menus. All the while, in the back of my mind, I was skeptical about whether it would truly happen.

"I think there's a right time for everything, and I'm a true believer that everything happens for a reason." –Bella Hadid

31

Nothing proves this more than when my husband ran into a former colleague and he told him about the coffee-shop plans. The colleague responded that he had just purchased a building in the Southampton Neighborhood of South City—one of the very neighborhoods we were targeting. He agreed to complete the build-out to our specifications and offered us an amazing contract. We accepted.

We had no official business plan, no bank loans or SBA backing. We just knew that this is what we wanted, where we wanted, and that we were going to make it happen one way or another. At that point things started moving at lightning speed. Within a few short months, the lease was signed and the build-out was completed. In the fall of 2018, Espresso Yourself Coffee & Café opened its doors. The weekend was a whirlwind, but it was beyond amazing. The Macklind Business District was hosting its annual Macklind Days street festival on Saturday and we held our Grand Opening on Sunday. In hindsight, it's probably best that it all happened so quickly as I'm quite certain that, if given the time to think, I would have second-guessed the decisions and found reason to not take such a gamble.

The response of our friends, family and surrounding neighbors was astonishing. The support we have received from the Business District and its members, as well as the neighborhood association, has been overwhelming. Since settling in, I have not questioned for one moment that we did the right thing!

They say it's risky to go into business with family. However, what makes the partnership that Jules and I have work so well is that we know our own, as well as each other's strengths. Jules thinks in colors and I think in numbers. She is a creative visionary who is always looking for the next great connection, concept, opportunity, or network. She handles our marketing and social media with natural ability. I take care of the not quite as glamorous, yet vital "business" stuff such as finances and reporting. We consult each other and discuss issues prior to making any major decisions; but ultimately, we each manage the roles in which our strengths reside.

Jules and I had a vision of a warm, comfortable, and inviting space where people could come to grab a great cup of coffee on the go, meet a friend or associate for a bite to eat, or linger with a latte and a good book. We saw Espresso Yourself Coffee & Café as a neighborhood staple. Whether it's through our guests who visit daily, the performers at our monthly open-mic nights, or relationships with our local suppliers, we know that we have more than succeeded in bringing this vision to life. From the moment they walk in, visitors can feel the love we have put into everything we do. Guests are welcomed into our coffee shop as they would be welcomed into our homes. Whether it's their first or their hundredth time, our desire is for everyone to feel like our guest and our friend. We've even witnessed neighbors meeting for the first time and building friendships through their visits.

With only a year under our belts, our business had grown nicely. But rather than sit back and simply enjoy what we had created, we decided to expand on our vision. We had received several requests to rent the shop for private events such as showers, birthday parties and art exhibits. Flattered that people loved our space so much, of course we agreed and thus began our event services business. From there we made the decision to take our show on the road. We sought out a way to bring our warm, comfortable, happy space to our guest's home, place of business, or event venue. With a little research, we realized there were very few specialty coffee shops that offered catering services. We found a need to be filled and felt we were just the ones to do it. Espresso Yourself Around Town is our mobile barista business that came to life in the summer of 2019 and is the focus of our growth in 2020 and beyond.

Looking back, I realize I had spent the first forty-some years of my life taking the logical and safe path. Creating Espresso Yourself Coffee & Cafe took a huge leap of faith for me. I may have been scared to death, but I believed in myself and my sister and what we envisioned. Even more so, I knew that together we could accomplish anything we put our heart and soul into. I would have to say it was probably the most *fearless* thing I have ever done or ever will do. Somehow, I managed to do it while maintaining my comfort zone. I still work my full-time job. I still try to live my version of a normal wife and mother: being home most evenings to cook dinner and attend school functions or sporting events. The fact that I have been able to successfully balance it all and remain sane makes me feel pretty darn *fabulous*.

Continued…

Tracy Calabro is the co-owner and Chief Happiness Junkie #2 of Espresso Yourself Coffee & Café in St Louis, MO. Tracy and her sister, Jules Karagiannis, opened their dream business in the fall of 2018. Together they built a simple "what-if" thought into a thriving neighborhood destination. Tracy and Jules opened their coffee shop to provide others with a safe and comfortable place to visit to celebrate with friends or to escape the craziness of the world.

Tracy primarily handles the financial side of Espresso Yourself Coffee & Café while she continues to work her full-time job as a Technical Communications & Marketing Coordinator at a locally owned chemical distribution company.

Above all else, Tracy's greatest accomplishments are being a wife and mother of four amazing humans. Her passions include caring for others and helping those in need.

Tracy Calabro
Chief Happiness Junkie #2
tracy@espressoyourselfcafe.com
www.espressoyourselfcafe.com
@espressoyourselfSTL
@es.presso_yourself
www.linkedin.com/in/dr-vivian-sierra-lmft-4621a23a/

Creating Change Later in Life

We are living in an unprecedented time in our lives. Turning 50 years old used to DREADED by our society, but today many are finding it is a time for a re-emergence and rejuvenation. We no longer see the latter part of our lives as something to just be tolerated or to watch the rest of our years pass by. We have been catapulted into a new age with new beliefs and it is high time we capitalize on these beliefs, ESPECIALLY if we are 50 years old or beyond.

The information age has brought with it many new beliefs and ways of thinking. It has modernized information. Communication processes have become the driving force of social evolution. Some of these beliefs cause us to take a close look at how our circumstances are created. Just recently for example with the Coronavirus, we are seeing the evidence of how our world has changed drastically. And the time to do the inner work and to understand that we live in more than one dimension has come.

Scientists and philosophers have shown us how any person can adopt the quantum model in our personal lives to effect change. And as a result, many do not theorize, but KNOW that anything is possible for us!

Although it is a sophisticated process on how all the energy works together to bring our outer circumstances to fruition, the simplified version is that we become what we think about all day long. This is why mindset has become such a hot topic of discussion and also become one of the most important things we as humans can study and apply. However, it is not JUST our mindset that we need to tend to in order to change our lives drastically. We need to understand that in order to make ANY change in our lives, we have to change our energy. For me, this involves getting in touch with who I really am.

We are God's highest form of creation and we have been blessed with the capability to alter and change our environment. We have been gifted with the ability to co-create with the sources in our world today. But we cannot use these gifts if we do not understand them. I went most of my life not understanding these concepts at all. For many of us, we have to have an incident that serves as a wakeup call to begin to understand we are the creators of our lives. My wakeup call came at the age of 47. I was faced with a divorce and found myself at the end of my rope. I needed help desperately.

I found help in two arenas. Around this time, I dove into a 12-step program of Recovery. I poured my heart and soul into the Principles of this program as if my life depended on it, because frankly it did. Through applying the steps, I started to see some of my patterns that were leading to results I did not want. I hired my first life coach at this same time and she began to change my ideas of who I was. I learned that I was a spiritual being in a physical body. I learned that I was a small, but important part of a much bigger Universe. I started using the ideas and tools she gave me and my life began to change drastically. Strange coincidences started showing up out of nowhere. Within just a few months, I had doubled my income and had more happiness than I thought was possible. I was meditating, investigating my past to see what my patterns were, showing up honestly and truly trying to do my best in everything. And life was so good!

I wanted to understand how my life had changed so quickly and dramatically. And since that is exactly what I went seeking, that is what I found! After studying with one of the leading authorities in personal development, Bob Proctor, I started to see the evidence of how our minds shape our reality. I was introduced to many people who were studying and applying this information. They told of the evidence in their lives and helped me understand the material a little better. One of my mentors and friends Dan Mangena, explains the phenomena in a very simple manner. "The mind does not lose, and your results do not lie," he says. What he means by this is that whatever idea is dominant in your subconscious mind will always show up as real results in your outer world.

So, what does this mean for us at the age of 50 or beyond? It means that we are turning 50 at one of the most exciting times in history EVER! It means that we can learn how to cultivate our thoughts and feelings in order to create the life we desire. It means we no longer have to be victims of the circumstances in our lives because we know that the outside circumstances are NOT where the creation process begins. We know the creation process begins inside.

We have to look at our lives in a very specific manner in order to decide what goals or aspirations are right for us to pursue. But where do we start? This is why I created the ABCD Method. It is exactly what you need to decide on what you want to create in your life. Below is an explanation of the program. It is easy to remember and apply!

ABCD Method:

A - Accept

B - Believe

C - Commit

D - Decide

A - Accept. The first thing you must do is to get really honest with yourself on two accounts: where you are and where you want to go. Start by making a list of where you are currently, all the facts in your life. Include the good and bad circumstances. Then, review what led you to your current situation. Note the patterns of what worked and what did not work.

Next, get honest about where you want to go. Without a vision or a plan, you won't get to where you want to go; you will wander. You have to know where you are going in order to follow the map. Take an inventory of ALL of your wants. What would you like to have MORE of in your life? What new things would you like to experience or do? Who do you want to BE in this world? Look at it ALL.

Look at different categories such as your health, relationships, and career. How would you like to spend your time? What would your career and finances look like? Where would you be living, who would you be living with, and what hobbies would you like to be involved in? What contribution would you like to make to society, your community, or your household? Once you have looked honestly at where you are, how you got there, and where you want to go, you are ready for the next step.

B - Belief. The next step is to adopt a new belief; for example, "No matter what has happened in the past or where I am right now, it is entirely possible for me to be, do, and have what I want." You MUST adopt the belief that you CAN do what you want! In order to do so, you need to get in touch with your deepest desires.

These desires are given to you for a REASON. Only you have these specific desires and only you have your unique way of looking at the world. These desires are pointing you where you need to go. So listen to them. Then BELIEVE that if God or the Universe gave you these desires, then They will definitely help guide you to them. Adopt this belief! Make it yours. Simplify it so you can remember it.

Here are a few examples of simplified versions of this belief.

-*"If I can see it in my mind, I can hold it in my hands."* Bob Proctor

-*"Everything is Figureoutable!"* Marie Forleo

-*"There is nothing impossible to him who will try."* Alexander the Great

-*"If you can dream it, you can do it."* Walt Disney

-*"I believe in the Miraculous."* Scott Haug

These quotes are NOT just for the people going for big things, they are for ALL of us. They are spoken by those who have gone before us to show us the way. Pick one belief that you want to adopt and write it down.

MY NEW BELIEF:_____

C - Commit. After you have decided on your new belief, the next step is to commit. Commit to doing the work no matter how long it takes to allow your dreams to come true. Your dreams are meant to come true! But they will only do so if you commit to the new belief AND take the necessary steps to allow your dreams to come about.

Action is key. But it is NOT just physical action you must take. You must take action on four levels. You will have to work on the spiritual, mental, emotional, and physical aspects of yourself. For this to happen, you need to be relaxed and open to new ideas, as well as, determined and disciplined. You must start working on these four levels however they present themselves at the time. This is where it is very helpful to have a mentor to guide you along this path. If you make the commitment to do the work, your teacher WILL appear.

If you are ready to commit, then write this statement down. "I, (your name), commit to doing the necessary work in order to make my dreams and deepest desires a reality in my life." Sign and date this and put it away somewhere.

You have accepted what you want, adopted a new belief, and made the commitment to do the work. Now the fun begins!

D - DECIDE. It is time to decide on which one of the dreams, visions, or desires you want to pursue first! Look at the list that you made in the Accept step and circle the one that makes you feel most alive! Then make a decision to go for it with everything you have inside of you! Write that goal on an index card, laminate it, and carry it with you everywhere you go. Keep it top of your mind. When you keep your goals top of your mind, it is easy to assess if what you are currently doing is in alignment with what you truly want to create. You will start to see the relationship between your thoughts, feelings and actions, and the outcomes you are producing in your life. Through constant self assessment, you can make the necessary changes to allow your dreams to come true! This is a great tool for starting you on your way to realizing your desires, putting the quantum model to work, and allowing what is meant for you to materialize.

I, for one, am so incredibly grateful and excited to be living my midlife and beyond right now! It is a blessing to be able to view these latter years of my life in an entirely new spirit, be ready to take on my world, and go for what I truly want. I am excited that we have so many individuals all over the world teaching this quantum model of living and being.

Change will begin to happen quite quickly in your life with consistent and dedicated action. In just 3 short years, my life has completely changed. I am living with purpose, passion, and a playfulness that excites me every day!

So, let's make a pact. No more excuses. No more guilt. No more doubt. You too CAN and WILL have the life you have so desired. There is no mistake. You are reading this today. You are ready. Take the first step.

Continued...

Barbara Joyce is a Women's Empowerment Coach. Following her passion in personal development, she empowers women to find their voices and take steps in creating the life they desire. No stranger to failure and disappointment, Barbara realizes much of being a coach is about lifting the client up and creating an atmosphere of trust. It is about expanding who they are as individuals to create a stronger bond with what they already know to be true inside. She knows from personal experience, that having that one person in life who we trust makes all the difference in the world. Barbara wants to be that person who guides her clients to freedom.

By creating an atmosphere of trust, Barbara helps women identify what pain points and obstacles inhibit them from achieving true freedom. By addressing these subconscious beliefs and habits, she helps clients create a stronger bond with their true selves and share their unique talents with the world. This results in ultimately freeing them to be not only who they want to be, but also who they are designed to be. Barbara believes that we all have a purpose and she is committed to helping each client find theirs.

iambarbarajoyce@gmail.com
www.barbarajoyce.com/coaching/
www.facebook.com/barbarajoyce.me/?modal=admin_todo_tour
www.instagram.com/barbarajoycelive/
www.twitter.com/babsjoyce
www.linkedin.com/in/barbara-joyce-23601712/

DANELLE BROWN

The Magic Of New Beginnings

Queen Bee Consulting was born in 2008—quite literally one of the worst times to open a company. I didn't know what was about to happen to the economy, and it is a good thing I didn't because I know I would have backed out. I had been marketing my then husband's technology company since 1997. I had no training, no coaching and absolutely no clue when it came to running a business. We had no business plan except that if we ran out of money, we would both go get our corporate jobs back. I decided to network like crazy. I went to every networking event I could find to grow our company. Without a store front—and no social media to speak of at that time—networking was the only way to get the word out that our company even existed. Along the way I picked up some business coaching certifications and started learning online marketing. By 2008 I created a d/b/a from our technology company that stemmed from my nickname, "Queen Bee of Networking." Little did I know that by 2012 I would be offering my skills to other companies to help them with their online marketing, and that is when Queen Bee really started to grow.

Between 2008 and 2012, home life was equally as crazy as work. We had two little girls. I was also balancing care-giving duties for my Mother who had multiple illnesses. It was very common for me to be pushing her in a wheelchair to medical appointments with my two little ones in tow, saddled down with purses, a laptop and a diaper bag.

We had taken on a brick and mortar store in 2008, and two years later we lost our shirts. Frankly, we lost everything. Not only did we close the store, but we lost our company structure, our home, our 401 Ks, and worst of all I lost faith in myself. Even though there were many people involved, and many decisions made,

I took on the full responsibility internally. To make matters even worse, not long after losing everything I also lost my biggest fan and the source of my strength: my Mother. Her death changed my entire world—and still does to this day.

I retreated. It was all I could do on a daily basis to keep showing up for my girls and doing what I had to do to rebuild our company and guard our reputations as much as possible. I solely existed by the "fake it till you make it" mentality. I did not allow myself to grieve the loss of our business or the loss of my mother appropriately for fear of losing what little I had left.

During that same time of immense struggle with the technology company, somehow Queen Bee was starting to grow. I was learning new coaching methods. I also was learning how to run social media for other businesses and was fortunate to be in the right place at the right time for this new world. I continued to learn and network, but this time both for the technology company we were trying to rebuild, as well as Queen Bee. Unfortunately, everything I had ever known since starting a business came to a screeching halt when I was faced with divorce.

My entire existence in the entrepreneurial world was tied to my now ex-husband and the company that I had worked so hard to build for so long. My reputation, my business, my face, my name, everything had always been tied to the technology company that was his name. This business that I had spent 20 years building was now gone.

As I always did, I put on a brave face and tried to keep promoting Queen Bee. For the first six months after the divorce, every time I went out to network, I was inevitably faced with having to explain not only the split of my marriage, but also how I was there only to represent Queen Bee Consulting. It was such a humiliating and painful experience that I stopped doing the very thing I loved most—i.e., networking and connecting people—out of sadness and fear.

What was I afraid of?

I was afraid of re-living what had happened to my family and the company every time I stepped outside.

I was afraid of losing Queen Bee due to what others thought of me. You never know how people will react to the news of a divorce. Especially when the two people ran a company together AND had shared clients. I never wanted to make anyone feel like they had to choose sides.

I was deeply afraid that providing for my two beautiful daughters solely rested on me doing a good job running Queen Bee. What if I failed? What would happen to us?

I also was running away from the fact that I had written a book about running a business with a spouse and staying married—something that took me years to finish and now obviously something I was not even able to do. I felt I could no longer have the title "Author" behind my name, which was heartbreaking considering all I had put into that project.

Since our company lost everything in 2010, I had been stuck in survival mode. All I did was react to what was being thrown at me instead of being pro-active to how I should be living my life and running my company. I would wake up every morning and just resign myself to being ready for the next disaster.

Then a great friend and supporter sent me a book that had really helped her during a rough time. It was *"More Language of Letting Go"* by Melody Beattie. I read a wonderful passage in the book that asked, "Do you want to be a thermometer or a thermostat? A thermometer simply tells you the temperature—a thermostat acknowledges what the temperature is, but then gives you the ability to do something about it." It was like someone slapped me in the face. I realized that I wanted to be a thermostat!

This was the slap in the face I needed. I knew I could be a thermostat. I knew I wanted to determine the course of my own actions and create a business and a life that I was proud of. I also knew I wanted to help others that were struggling and to share what I had learned through my journey. It was time for me to step back into my power and my confidence.

It has been two years since I read that passage, two years of learning lessons and two years of finding the guts to speak publicly about it. So, now, I share with you what I have learned, in hopes that it may help you or that you can pass it on to someone else who may be going through a rough time . . .

1. **You own your knowledge**. Thankfully, my attorney told me this very wise piece of advice back when we first lost our shirts and he was helping me with all the legal paperwork to start over. He assured me no matter what I was going through financially, nothing could take away the knowledge that I had gained. I would still know how to market. I would still know

how to help my clients. The same is with you, whatever your profession. Nothing that is happening could ever take the knowledge from your brain.

2. **It is not a bad thing to take time for yourself**. You do not have to be constantly working to prove yourself to anyone. If you don't give yourself a minute just to breathe, you will never catch your breath. Or worse yet, your body will make you take care of yourself at the most inopportune time.

3. **Pay it forward**. I was so thankful for friends who reached out with kind words, supportive advice, or books that had helped them through tough journeys. Consider ordering books or sharing websites so you can share with others what you learned while you were going through some tough times.

4. **If you don't have faith in yourself, why should you expect other people to?** Even if you have not learned to embrace faith over fear, even when new things scare the hell out of you, give it time. After all, you have made it this far, so your track record is pretty good!

5. **Get comfortable with being uncomfortable**: I recall this advice that I was given by my original coach, Michael Port, author of *Book Yourself Solid*. No growth has ever come out of staying in your comfort zone, and it certainly doesn't come from playing it safe.

6. **Do NOT run away**. You worked hard for your knowledge AND your reputation. NO ONE can take that away from you. NO ONE.

7. **Ask for help**. This does not make you weak. There are many things about running a business that I still need help with, such as financial decisions. It took me a long time to realize that asking for help is not a sign of weakness, but actually a wise decision for accepting what my strengths are and what they are not—and then going to find the right people who have those strengths that I lack. It was then that I was able to move on to what I was good at. Don't be afraid—ask for help.

8. **You are just as important as your clients**. Your company cannot grow if you are constantly focused on only your clients, and not putting enough energy towards your own growth and continued education.

9. **Always remember the "Red Velvet Rope."** The Red Velvet Rope was the first lesson I was taught and now teach to my coaching clients from the *Book Yourself Solid* system that I mentioned before. It means to be

selective of your clients and only work with the people that energize and inspire you to do your best work. This means you are not meant to work with everyone. You are not everyone's cup of tea, and they are not necessarily yours. Don't take on clients just for the sake of the work. Do what motivates you to do your best. Don't be afraid to say NO.

10. **Be more vocal about what energizes and inspires you**, and do not be afraid of going after what you truly love to do. Get out of survival mode and stop taking any gig that comes along just to "pay the bills." When a new client comes along, one of the first questions should be, "Is this going to be fun?" Life is too short not to have fun.

11. **Visualize and EXPECT exactly what you want**. Mindset is everything, but you need to be specific with what you want. This goes beyond saying to yourself a blanket term like "I want to be successful," and being more SPECIFIC of what that looks like for you. How many more clients? How much more money exactly? What source does it come from? This goes for personal expectations as well. Just like you expect the sun to rise every day, you have to expect that your hard work and intentions will pay off.

12. **We are all a work in progress**. I will be honest. I am still learning the art of letting go of a life that is gone and embracing the possibilities of what lies ahead now that I make all the rules. I am definitely not perfect, and still find myself repeating some old behaviors. The same is with you. You cannot expect to undo habits and thought patterns from the last 20 years overnight, so learn to give yourself some grace, but also push yourself forward even when you are scared to go that direction.

My advice to anyone reading this chapter is: You are not alone. We all have our personal struggles, worries or fears, and I know for a fact that everyone doubts themselves at some point for some reason. Find yourself some support. Find new cheerleaders, I guarantee they are out there.

Melody Beattie is also known for saying, "Letting go of our ideas about how life should go is a choice that sets life's magic free."

Here's to letting go—and to the magic of new beginnings!

Continued…

Danelle Brown is the founder and CEO of Queen Bee Consulting, a marketing and communications agency which she started in October of 2008. She is a Certified Book Yourself Solid Business Coach, and a Certified Asset Based Thinking Coach.

Danelle began her career as a professional business coach, but quickly used her skills and talents to help her clients promote themselves online. Her specialties are using any and all of her skills to help her clients shine. This includes harnessing the power of YouTube and video—the next best thing to being there in person—as well as discovering the best social media platform for each customer's business.

Danelle also consults with clients on the importance of email marketing, proper website design, and how to utilize their social capital through networking.

www.queenbeeconsulting.com
dbrown@queenbeeconsulting.com
www.facebook.com/QueenBeeConsulting/
www.twitter.com/DanelleBrown
www.linkedin.com/in/danellebrown

LORI HENSON

Leaving the Passenger Seat

Let's be clear. This isn't a story written by an expert in changing one's life. Keep looking if that's your quest and I wish you well. This is a story of my journey, fumbling and flawed as it was, but guided by what I'm certain is a divine power. I had thought my choices were pathways out of difficult situations. It turned out they were a way through to a part of me I didn't know existed.

In 1998, I was enthralled in a career that I fell into. In my youth, I didn't say "I want to be a _____ " and then dedicate myself to that purpose. I was good at math and science and a high school counselor said I should be an engineer....so of course that's what I did. After five years in college in a very difficult curriculum, I had my first identifier: Engineer.

Now what? Well, I took the first job I could get, learned new skills, moved on and established myself as one of a very few female construction professionals. That's a whole book in itself, but let's just say it wasn't easy. I had no mentors to help me and felt very alone. But I survived, reputation intact, and glided into middle age confident in nothing. Well not nothing. One thing was certain. I hated my career.

When I say hated, here's an example. On several occasions, I narrowly avoided high speed collisions on my way to work. At those moments, I thought "I should have let the car hit me, I wouldn't have to go to work today." These are tragic memories, even years later. But here's the thing. Those moments were gifts! What was to come brought clarity in a way I never expected.

One night after a particularly stressful day, I came home as I've done before, my first stop being my bedroom where I cried my eyes out for an hour before sliding ungracefully into the role of mother and wife. On this night, I looked upward and said "God, I can't do this anymore." Something happened that shocked and scared me. I clearly heard "You don't have to." My tears and sobs immediately stopped. I sat up and said, "What just happened?" I kept this experience a secret for fear of being judged, but it never left my mind.

For a few years, I tried different employers and roles, searching for the fulfillment that was lacking. But two new jobs and seven long years from God speaking to me, nothing had changed. I was still experiencing the same sense of dread in my daily life. Add to that some new problems: my father's diagnosis of Alzheimer's disease and my own heart problems due to work stress. I began wondering if I'd ever be happy again. I was in a very dark place and, quite scared. Too many things were out of my control. Or so I thought.

My father's passing in early 2006 forced me to take stock of my life. You see, he also hated his career. I started to realize there was a strong likelihood that stress led to his depression, dependence on multiple prescriptions, dementia, and ultimately Alzheimer's. I had the opportunity to break that chain and show my two sons that they could navigate their lives and careers and not feel stuck. I wanted to be an example. And more than anything, I wanted to see what would happen if I listened to those words in my head from all those years before that told me "you don't have to." I made the choice to let the exploration begin.

Have no doubt, I was afraid. I kept my secret very private, only telling my husband and one or two friends. At the age of 46, I was finally ready to see what my destiny could be with my own happiness in mind rather than sticking to what I knew or what was expected of me.

A month later, we got a call from a financial advisor proposing an initial meeting. We'd never had financial advice before, but even with our crazy schedules, something told us to take the meeting. And I was curious where it would lead. Perhaps I could have someone take some responsibility off my shoulders.

The first meeting was straight forward: Current situation, goals, financial numbers. Nothing earth shattering but I found it impactful and saw where continued conversations could help.

The second meeting was supposed to be the analysis and recommendations he'd prepared. But I threw him a curve when I said that I was leaving my career in the next six months before it had a chance to kill me. From my demeanor, he could tell I was serious. This led to a question I hadn't ever asked myself. "What do you want your day to be like?" After a few seconds, I listed off the first stream of consciousness that hit me. I wanted:

- to help people.
- to be in control of my day.
- to achieve my full potential.

Well you can likely guess the rest. After several months of interviews, soul searching and tests, I left the construction industry behind and started life anew. I'd lost my original identifier, that of engineer, and had taken on a new identifier, that of financial advisor.

This new role was intellectually challenging for sure, but also spiritually taxing. With every obstacle, I thought I had misinterpreted God's words and maybe this wasn't His plan for me.

One tragic obstacle to building my new business was the death of my mother, eight months into this new career. She died unexpectedly and while I won't divulge what happened, I will say that it caused a post-traumatic stress disorder of sorts, leading to months of panic attacks and fear. I was grappling not only with the cause of her death, but also the realization that I wasn't a daughter anymore. The loss of that identifier, daughter, became a struggle that forced me into therapy and a journey of self-awareness and vulnerability, things I'd always avoided.

I decided to trust my mentors and friends who told me I had what it took to succeed as a financial advisor. I trusted clients who said I was helping them (one even called me her angel). But mostly I trusted that God put me right where I was meant to be. I just had to keep trusting, one day at a time. I let my vulnerability show and clients gravitated toward the reality that they could trust me because I was real.

Now for the next transition that I never saw coming. I'd made several wonderful friends in this new career, many of them much younger than me. One good friend was getting married and asked me to write something to read at her wedding because my husband and I had the type of marriage they wanted. No pressure, right?

One Sunday night, I was getting ready for bed and decided to compose a poem that I'd hoped would say what they were looking for. Little did I know that the next phase of my awakening was taking root.

The initial shock of that first foray into writing poetry was the complete ease of words flowing from my mind to the page. I got into a head space where I thought of past loves of this couple, but also of my own relationships, and those of my children as they found their ways to true love. The title "Love Waits" started a stream of consciousness poem that had rhyme, cadence, beginning, middle and end, and to this day, I've never changed a word from the original writing.

Although it was very positively received by the couple, I was shaking like a leaf in a wind storm as I stood at the church altar, outwardly expressing what had come to me in that quiet moment months prior. Yes, I was nervous and afraid, but also guided. I knew in my soul that I was saying words that would resonate with others. I received instant confirmation as I returned to the pew, seeing tears rolling down not only my husband's face but several others as well, strangers who had no idea who I was or what to expect as I stood there vulnerable and terrified.

The second shock was the realization that I was seeing poetry and prose in everyday life. Something opened in my spirit that let me see the world differently, hear stories more poignantly, and find a way to transfer those experiences to the written page. Just like the first time I wrote that Sunday night, the words flowed quite effortlessly. Afterward I had no idea how I created them. It was quite overwhelming. More than once, I became anxious that I was heading down a path towards something completely foreign but compelling all the same.

Fast forward several years and dozens of poems later, I found myself questioning what I was meant to do with these pieces that I was spiritually guided to compose. Was I prepared to add an identifier, that of published author? As a test, I shared the poems with friends and posted some on social media. The response was always overwhelmingly positive. "You need to publish these!" was something I heard so often that I finally realized that I needed to get out of my own way and start exploring that possibility. Could I do this? More importantly, should I do this?

A few things happened relatively quickly in the summer of 2018. The sudden tragic deaths of two women I knew forced me to realize that time was precious.

We aren't guaranteed tomorrow. I wrote a poem to console the husband of one of those friends, and when he told me it was the most beautiful thing he'd ever read, I knew what I had to do. I thought of a future where my sons and husband were at my funeral, friends asking them why I had never done anything with my poetry and what a shame it was that I was too afraid to explore possibilities.

That did it. I very selectively told close family and friends of my writing project, and because the Universe sometimes rewards patience, I began meeting the people who would help turn my plans into reality. I used my lifetime love of photography and decided to combine those two creative elements for the most impact. I published my poetry and photography book only five months after the initial contact with my design team. It was scary, thrilling, time-consuming, and overwhelming. Happily, I am forever changed because I stepped out onto that ledge supported by love, faith, and a future vision more expansive than I'd dreamt possible. I felt whole.

My hope is that you identify with my fears and uncertainties. I want you to find the courage to reach into your inner core, compelled by forces beyond your understanding. You will perhaps explore some painful truths; and with painful clarity as your reward, you'll grow in ways you never imagined.

Upon reflection, I learned valuable lessons. I wasn't meant to live life paralyzed by fear, enabling regret to take root in my soul. We're all meant to explore, share, grow and hopefully feel compelled to make changes that get us closer to our truest selves, regardless of how others identify or limit us.

I also learned that when broken down, the word "disease" really means dis-ease, living in a way that inhibits growth and happiness. Perhaps like me, you're hiding your truest self and finding that your rewards are sleepless nights, anxiety, over indulging, and denial.

Through these lessons, I created a new identifier for myself—that of poet and author—one that is free of my father's legacy of regret and suffering. I liberated myself (and hopefully my sons) from living in the passenger seat of life.

I wish you joy as your own identity exploration begins.

Continued…

Lori Henson has experienced several identifiers in her life, one leading to another, on a path she didn't foresee. As an Engineer, construction Project Manager, and Financial Advisor, she has learned how to listen and solve problems with a goal in mind.

Along the way, she became aware of a talent she had never tapped into. With urging from family and friends, she explored her creative side. She used her listening skills to translate stories and observations into poetry. An author was born. Often emotional, Lori's poems elicit praise from those she shares them with individually and through social media.

Today, she still advises clients on their financial matters but now sees a future for herself as a writer who combines the visual beauty of her landscape photography with impactful poetry and prose.

Through her book, "Love Waits: Imagery and Prose to Celebrate, Console and Inspire," readers enjoy spectacular full color photographs taken in National Parks and several countries, with dozens of heartfelt poems that are sure to inspire.

Lori is a wife, mother, and grandmother who lives in St. Louis, MO.

Love Waits is available on Amazon, or for or a personalized, signed hardback copy, go to www.throughmyeyespress.com.

InstaGram is Through My Eyes Press (username is throughmyeyespress)
Facebook is facebook.com/throughmyeyespress
Website is www.throughmyeyespress.com
Email is throughmyeyespress@gmail.com

Illimitable!

"You are not your body" I heard her words yet I wasn't making sense of what she was saying. She repeated, "You are not your body." This time she continued, "When you told me that you had been held captive yet the thought that you might have been killed had never crossed your mind, I knew you knew. You are not your body—you are spirit. That is who you really are. Nothing can take that from you."

Amid jumbling flashes of memories, I began to reconstruct the preceding days. I was a commercial real estate broker and only occasionally, under special circumstances, did I take residential referrals. Thinking it would be a good contact for me, a friend of a friend had suggested that I meet with the owner of some resort properties who was considering selling his "cabin nestled in the woods." Cabin was an understatement. It was a large residence secluded deep in the Tahoe National Forest several miles of dirt road from the highway.

I had called ahead to let him know that I was running late and to confirm that he still wanted to meet. When I arrived 30 minutes late, he came out to the car and was overly gracious. Inside the house, he offered me some wine. I said I preferred to start by looking at his beautiful home. He insisted so I took the glass. His gracious demeanor started degrading rapidly. It became apparent that he was furious. I suggested that I should leave. He became enraged, stomping and ranting room to room. The mood swings were enormous: alternating without warning between politely insisting that I have more wine and railing at me knocking the glass out of my hand, spraying wine in all directions. As the glass shattered on the tile floor, my mind raced, imagining how to get out of the house.

When he noticed that I was positioning myself closer to the door, it triggered another outburst, "What makes bitches like you think you can get away with luring men on and then playing games." I tried to make a break for the door. My hair was very long and pulled back with an elastic. He grabbed my hair and threw me to the floor. The more I tried to sooth his anger, the angrier he became. Much of what ensued is still a blur—the mind induces situational amnesia to shield us from some things. I remember biting him and him hitting me in the face. He raped me and then fell on top of me in a drunken stupor. I managed to squirm out from under him. He didn't waken. I snuck out of the room, grabbing my things.

I ran bare foot across pine needles and pebbles. Arriving at my car, I realized I had left a jacket. Demonstrating how totally irrational I was, I felt I had to remove everything of me from that place. I ran back to the house, snuck in, grabbed my jacket and ran even faster back to the car and hit the auto-lock. A thought flashed that he might dash out of the house in front of the car. I imagined accelerating right into him. I have wondered since if I actually could have done that.

With tears blurring my vision, I drove as fast as I could down the forest road to the highway. I was terrified that he might have tried to follow me. I swung onto the highway and drove until I saw a neon sign. It was a convenience store. I stumbled my way in. The clerk said, "Oh my God!" and wrapped me in a blanket. It smelled like cigarette smoke; I didn't care. The police came; I felt like I was watching SVU on television. The tears came in batches. Thoughts swirled. I don't remember how I got to the hospital or how my car got to the hospital or when Nancy, an amazing young woman, who was there to be my advocate, joined us.

In the examination room there were nurses firing all sorts of questions at me including asking if it was okay if an officer (male) remained in the room while they collected evidence including photographs. I was so muddled. I thought I was supposed to be cooperative—"be nice" —like in the intruding flashes of my childhood. Later at the trial, the defense attorney, pointing to my smile in one of those embarrassing pictures from the emergency room, claimed I was just fine that all that happened was consensual.

The next morning, I insisted I was okay. In spite of Nancy's objections, they released me from the hospital to drive home alone. It was a mistake. I wasn't okay. Between trying to breathe through the sobbing that started the moment I was in the car, see through tears and think through the jumbled thoughts, suddenly I was feeling everything I felt when fleeing down the dirt road from the man's house. They should have insisted on calling someone to come for me.

Careening through an array of emotions, I grappled with instant replays of violence and captivity interjected with swells of feeling grounded—being okay deep inside, in spite of everything. Soothing waves washed over me knowing I had "my team." The first person I called was my minister, it was her reassuring voice that carried me through to unveiling my new identity. I was not my body. Nothing that had happened to my body could diminish the real me.

Nancy, my angel-advocate, who companioned me through all the weirdness, stayed in my life years beyond the trial. The lead detective, Chris, who let me know at the hospital that they had arrested the man, kindly, didn't mention the number of unsecured, loaded guns they had found in the house until much later. Among the traumas within the trauma was Chris's fatal heart attack shortly before the trial. I not only grieved the loss of someone who had become my friend, but feared the inability of others to make sure the man could not harm anyone else. My team was filled out with the women who came forward after reading the newspaper account and testified at the trial that he had raped them, too.

I can attest to how traumatic a trial can be for an assault victim. I was so terrified of facing the man that I relived the whole experience and began to doubt every memory to the point of believing the defense that I had made the whole thing up. Shame is so peculiar—a tangle preventing me to "admit" what happened—not even to those closest to me—my daughter, my business partner, gal-friends with whom I had shared my life over many years. Some people called me a "very private person"—I was actually a very ashamed person. I had a storehouse of memories I judged to be unacceptable. I was good at maintaining my façade.

Many years ago, John Powell wrote a book, *Why Am I Afraid to Tell You Who I Am.* My answer was easy, "Because if you knew, you (like many of your predecessors) would throw me away." I didn't know that those predecessors probably threw me away because they felt that I would not let them know me. They probably felt rejected. I felt abandoned which only further reinforced my other-than-conscious belief that a façade was my only way to survive. I am blessed that along the way some people saw through that façade and loved me anyway.

55

My conscious decision to not be defined by the event—my decision to thrive rather than merely survive—set the emerging me in motion. I had been broken open like Humpty-Dumpty and I couldn't be put back together again—which was a very good thing. What shone through the cracks was amazing. Knowing that nothing in the physical world could damage or diminish me, I was free to experiment with letting my light shine. Although hesitant, I understood that thriving involves connections, relationships and authenticity with the accompanying vulnerability. I was hesitant and fear pulled me back, yet the lure of new possibilities pushed me out of my shell. I understood Anais Nin's, "*And the day came when the risk to remain tight in a bud was more painful than the risk it took to blossom.*" I was in a prison of my own making. Suddenly, the prison doors flung open. I was free to let go of being acceptable and embrace being authentic. What a concept!

Sadness washed over me for having "unlived" my life and then I remembered, "it's never too late to start again." Wow! I had found my launching pad—I was a living analogy of peeling an onion—peel a layer, shed a lot of tears, reveal more layers, resist further peeling in fear of pain, remember the pain of staying stuck, arise and refuse to further perpetuate the lies I had been living, recommit to continue—no matter what.

Some said my experience was awful. Perception controls how we experience every situation. Our beliefs control our perceptions—particularly our beliefs about ourselves. Those beliefs dictate whether our outcomes are lasting or fleeting, negative or positive. We are collages—assemblages of thoughts—that have imprisoned or empowered us.

This experience was incredibly valuable. My refusal to be defined by the event forced me to embrace it rather than try to reject or deny it. Either of which could have caused me to be its emotional victim. Mulling over all that had happened, I heard myself singing some lines from the song "For Good"

> ... *people come into our lives for a reason*
> *Bringing something we must learn*
> *And we are led*
> *To those who help us most to grow*
> *If we let them*

And we help them in return
Well, I don't know if I believe that's true
But I know I'm who I am today
Because I knew you...
Who can say if I've been changed for the better?
But because I knew you
I have been changed for good

I'm still peeling the onion, discovering and uprooting the tendrils that had limited the full expression of me. I have committed to staying awake so old habits cannot reinstall themselves, and to leaning into and practicing being alive in each moment, remembering:

- Nothing can happen to my physical form that can damage or diminish the Truth. I am the pure, perfect potentiality of Spirit expressing as this particular form.
- The comments and opinions of others' about how I might look or act has nothing to do with me unless for some insane reason I agree. They belong to the critic and such a negative viewpoint only constricts the criticizer.
- Thriving requires self-acceptance and self-forgiveness for all the times I took on someone else's beliefs about me or felt hurt by someone's words or actions.

The thought of unlimited possibilities, complete with full responsibility (oh, my!), was astounding! How was I to select how this new me was going to be?

I took the liberty to make Etienne de Grellet's poem my own:

I shall pass this way but once.
Any change I can make or good that I can do,
let me do it now.
I shall not defer nor neglect it,
for I shall not have this moment again.

So, in each of these moments that I do have, I am committed to do my part to serve, uplift and empower others—to remind all that they are each pure, perfect spiritual potential not limited by their physical experiences. I am here to support them awakening to their illimitable life!

Continued...

Therisia "Trish" Hall, M.Div., an insightful internationally acclaimed, speaker and author, is the visionary Spiritual Leader of Center for Spiritual Living Metro which serves the Greater Washington DC Metro area.

In furtherance of her passion for peace and commitment to inclusivity, she founded Way2Peace, an organization dedicated to honoring the dignity of all life and expanding experiences of kindness and respect by facilitating the release of prejudices and other limiting beliefs. She is a member of the Fairfax County Interfaith Clergy Council and Interfaith Council of Washington, DC, as well as a founding member of Tysons Interfaith.

An outstanding educator, facilitator, and dedicated student of world philosophies, Trish has an innate ability to recognize commonalities and enhance communication among diverse populations which has positioned her as a presenter at the Parliament of World Religions and a panelist at World Association of Religions for Peace events.

Blending authenticity, humor and compassion, whether addressing an audience or working with individual clients in her private practice, she thrives on awakening the unique magnificence within all.

trishhall.unltd@gmail.com
www.trishhallunltd.com
www.cslmetro.org
www.way2peace.org
www.artofliving.com

Radical Acceptance

"Radical acceptance rests on letting go of the illusion of control and a willingness to notice and accept things as they are right now without judging." Marsha M. Linehan.

When I was three years old, I entered my first beauty pageant. I practiced smiling, walking down the runway and standing with my feet in semi-third position. The night before my mom had rolled up my long brown hair in soft, pink foam curlers that I slept in all night. The day of the pageant I wore a beautiful pink dress with white Mary Jane patent leather shoes. My hair flowed down my shoulders and back in perfect ringlet curls. That glorious day I earned the title, "Best Three-Year-Old." I also learned a lesson I would carry with me throughout my adult life—appearance is EVERYTHING!

I danced, sang, and acted from preschool through college with a few beauty pageants sprinkled in, which basically meant my entire childhood and early adult years were focused on what my face and body looked like. It was natural for me to be overly self-critical. I wasn't even aware I was doing it. Did I mention I was a chubby kid? Definitely a drawback when you're a dancer. My dream was to be on Broadway, but the harsh reality of having a not-so-dancer-like body caught up with me in my early 20s, so I decided to leave the music theater and dance world behind and become an educator where my appearance didn't matter.

I stayed in the education field for 15 years until I felt called to help others in a different way. I earned my health and life coach certifications, took a fearless leap of faith and started my own coaching business, Rise Up and Live Wellness, a name chosen because at one point that is exactly what I needed to do. I needed to rise up and live! I was alive and breathing, but more along the lines of striving, surviving and putting undue stress upon myself. I was living under society's standards and not being true to myself. Have you ever done that? Have you ever put so much pressure on yourself that your stress level was through the roof?

For the majority of my life, starting at age 10, I was a dieter. As a dancer I was expected to look a certain way; diets were a part of life. Over the years I became a professional yo-yo dieter—losing weight, finding it, losing weight, finding it. At the age of 39, I decided enough was enough. I was going to enter the next decade of my life skinny! After all, appearance was everything!

Have you ever set a goal for yourself which started out small and innocent, then snowballed out of control—like it just took on a mind of its own—until you found yourself out of control and no longer recognizing yourself? That's exactly what happened to me.

Like all dieters, I began restricting my calories. I was planning my meals and food prepping like a champ. Since I was already exercising, I decided a little more exercise would speed up my results. Who doesn't love instant gratification? I worked out longer and harder. The scale was going down and my clothes were getting loose. I looked good, but not good enough. I continued restricting the calories and over-exercising until I finally achieved my thinnest weight EVER. And I mean EVER! I was so excited! However, when I looked in the mirror, I still saw all my imperfections, like the extra fat under my arms and my disproportionate body. My body was nowhere near perfect like the models in the magazines or the actresses in Hollywood, so I continued to strive for perfection.

Turns out no matter how hard I tried my body had other plans for me. I was in adrenal fatigue, and my hormone levels and blood work were extremely low. I was stressed, exhausted, and unable to concentrate for long periods of time. I had to take long naps in the afternoon because I couldn't keep my eyes open. Not only was my body shutting down, I was emotionally defeated. I had worked so hard to lose weight and be skinny. I couldn't wrap my head around why this was happening to me when I had done what I thought was "right" — eat less, exercise more.

Turns out those warning signals were my body's way of getting my attention to rest and heal. WHAT? I didn't know how to rest and heal. I was a go-getter, type A, high-performer and perfectionist. Resting and relaxing meant being lazy! If I took time to rest and relax, what would happen to my body? What would happen to all my hard work?

I swallowed my pride and rested as I was told. Want to know what happened? I gained weight. Yep, I said it. I also gained energy, my stress level decreased, my sleep improved, and my ability to focus and concentrate increased. In fact, my health was the best it had been in years. However, I had to face the fact that my body was never going to look as "good" as it once did. This was HARD. Why? Because of shame. The entire time I was losing weight I received compliment after compliment. People were impressed with my discipline and willpower. Living in a thin body was like winning an Academy Award. I was accepted and fit into society.

On the other hand, gaining weight was shameful. I felt judged. I assumed people thought I was eating fast-food and dessert all day long. When in reality, I was feeding my body the food it had been deprived, the food it needed to restore my health. I continued to carry the shame and guilt because I deeply cared about what other people thought of me. Appearance was everything! I did not want to be judged and scrutinized by others.

It was during this time I made the decision to rise up and live. I had to start loving and accepting myself exactly as I was each day. I had to learn to love and accept all of my flaws, just as I loved my strengths. I had to learn how to look in the mirror without the Itty-Bitty-Shitty-Committee telling me how big my thighs looked, how I was a failure for gaining weight, and how I no longer looked cute in clothes. I had to look at my body in a neutral way that had nothing to do with its size. I had to retrain my brain to see the power I had in my legs that allowed me to run, squat, and dance. I had to appreciate how useful my arms were for hugging my family and completing everyday tasks. No judgement, only appreciation.

I also had to let go of what other people thought of me and focus instead on what I thought of myself. I had to release a big limiting belief: The belief that I had to be thin to be successful and accepted. This belief I learned as a child, appearance is everything, no longer served me. I had to replace the negative thoughts of "You're too fat," "You're not pretty enough," and "You're not good enough," with "Your body is healthy and strong," "You are unique and beautiful" and "You are enough." I had to dig deep to radically accept my body and my life. I had to surrender to the moment and practice being present with my feelings.

I can honestly say this is one of the greatest and most important things I've ever done for myself. By surrendering the control and learning how to love myself as I am, my relationships, business, health, and life have become fuller, richer and more enjoyable. I am now fully present in my daily life because I'm no longer consumed with how I look, how much fat, carbs, and protein I've had for the day and how many calories I've burned. I have mental space for things that truly matter in my life like my family, friends, clients, and serving others.

For me being fearless and fabulous means radically loving and accepting myself exactly as I am today. That is how I Rise Up and Live each day!

7 Ways to Radically Love and Accept Yourself

1. Let go of comparison and judgment.

Judging and comparing ourselves to others or our own expectations results in one of two things: an inflated or deflated ego. We quickly become "OK" with ourselves because we're better than or "not okay" because we're less than. When in reality, we're okay, we're enough, and we're acceptable as we are today. When we accept our weaknesses and flaws, as we accept our strengths, we realize they do not define us but make us unique and individual.

2. Release Limiting Beliefs.

Hanging onto old, outdated beliefs we learned as a child holds us back from true acceptance. Once we identify our limiting beliefs, appreciate the learnings and discover new beliefs which better serve us, we can move forward with a new perspective. Uncovering and releasing limiting beliefs is both life changing and empowering.

3. Forgive yourself.

When I ask my clients who they need to forgive, it is most often themselves. Why? Because they put an unnecessary amount of pressure on themselves to be right, better than or perfect. Their repeated criticisms and harsh words are on replay. We are our own worst critics. However, no one can take away our right to love and accept ourselves. No one, especially not us! When we forgive ourselves for past mistakes, love and acceptance flow into our being.

4. Be present.

When we focus on the past (should have, would have, could have), we're not present. When we're worried about the future (what if), we're not present. Being present is being completely in the moment, having our thoughts and attention on what is happening now. Focusing on our breath brings us back to the present moment.

5. Say daily affirmations.

Fill your mind with positive thoughts. Henry Ford said, "Whether you think you can or you think you can't, you're right." Become aware of your thoughts. Take captive any negative thoughts and put them on trial. Question if the negative thoughts are really true or if you are replaying something you were told when you were a child. Say positive affirmations each morning and night, such as "I love and accept myself as I am."

6. Adopt an attitude of gratitude.

Fear, anxiety, worry, and self-doubt diminish when your focus shifts to gratitude. Gratitude helps us focus on who we are and what we have, as opposed to what we lack. What qualities and experiences are you grateful for? Who are you grateful for in your life?

7. Surrender.

Surrendering is not giving up. Surrendering is accepting what is, accepting ourselves just as we are, without judgment. Surrendering doesn't mean we have to physically, mentally or emotionally stay where we are, it means we accept reality and then choose how to move forward, one step at a time. The practice of surrendering, when done intentionally and daily, provides an empowering and welcoming sense of freedom and peace.

We are each one-of-a-kind. We are each unique. Yes, we have flaws, flaws we get to accept and appreciate. If we don't love and accept ourselves as we are right this minute, we will not love and accept ourselves once we make more money, lose weight, start a career, get a promotion, fall in love, have children, and lose more weight. Instead, we will be on the hamster wheel of life trying to fill a hole deep within our soul, which in essence, can be filled right this moment with radical acceptance.!

Continued...

Kelli Risse, owner of Rise Up and Live Wellness, is a speaker, educator, and coach. Her passion is providing tools, support and accountability for busy professional women through her two signature coaching programs: "Practicing Peace" and "Make Peace with Food and Your Body." As a business owner, wife and mother, Kelli understands the chaos of living a stressful life. She uses master coaching techniques and her personal story to help women experience peace and live in optimal health.

Kelli is a Certified Neuro-Linguistic Programming (NLP) trainer, Certified NLP Master Coach, Certified TCM (Transformational Coaching Method) Master Coach, and Certified ICF Health & Life Coach. Kelli is a former National Board Certified educator. She has a BFA from Illinois Wesleyan, MFA from University of California, Irvine and a teaching certification from University of Denver.

Kelli grew up in St. Louis County, Missouri; she also lived in California and Colorado before returning to Missouri. In addition to her business, Kelli loves professional development, jazzercise, yoga, hanging out with friends, and the St. Louis Blues.

www.riseupandlivewellness.com
www.linkedin.com/riseupandlivewellness
www.facebook.com/riseupandlivewellness
www.instagram.com/kelli_risse
kelli@riseupandlivewellness.com

Tic, Tic, Boom – Fabulous

I realized that I regretted attending law school in my second year. Being a naive 23-year-old, I was convinced that I had reached a point of no return: I had no choice but to finish to earn a salary high enough to pay off my student loans. Things didn't turn out as planned, though, as I developed a passion for criminal prosecution, one of the least lucrative areas of law.

As a prosecutor, I was proud to fight against the most heinous crimes, sexual assaults and homicides, while making less money than my husband did with just a high school diploma. Despite my law-school ideas, I hadn't dedicated myself to this career for the money, but for the emotional rewards. My days consisted of hearing children retell the worst circumstances imaginable. Their stories filled me with compassion and protectiveness for them and a ferociousness in the courtroom, showing no mercy to the guilty. Being a champion for the harmed became a passion that drove me to put in 70 hours a week, oblivious to my failing physical and mental health from the overwhelming stress.

The pressure continued to build until it was time for extreme action—that is, moving from a career fighting for justice to fighting for fitness. I'd dreamt of owning a business for most of my adult life and had dabbled in a few money-making hobbies, like kickboxing instruction, so the switch to gym ownership wasn't as unusual as it seemed. I envisioned working with healthy, happy people, making my own schedule, earning unlimited income, and building a better life for my family. I felt no fear.

Applying the same work-ethic that had made me a force in the courtroom, I dived in—tackling every aspect of operations from training clients to selling memberships, designing marketing campaigns to administrative and accounting tasks. By working 70+ hours a week as the sole employee of our first retail fitness location, we were able to become profitable and hire our first part-time employee in just three months—yet, somehow, my hours did not decrease. Although it was exhausting and stressful, changing our members' lives for the better and positively impacting the community kept our spirits up and resulted in record growth—expanding to four locations in less than three years.

Outwardly, we were winning awards and being recognized in national publications, which reinforced that my approach to business was working. Little did I know—I was operating as an employee rather than the entrepreneur I had imagined. Three years in, I was at the gym over 12 hours a day while my husband worked full-time for a utility company and handled our household affairs. When I got home, I had just enough energy to eat a re-heated dinner while checking emails and posting on social media until falling into bed exhausted. I was so preoccupied with succeeding in order to get us to the life we deserved that I missed how much our relationship was suffering. We had dreamed of owning a business to have more time together and to indulge in our passion of traveling; yet there we were, five years since a vacation.

My husband gave me the wake-up call I needed with three little words—"I'm not happy." I'll never forget the chill that ran through me hearing him speak as I stood in the kitchen after another long day at the gym. "Do you want a divorce?" I asked. "No," he said, and my heart started beating again. "I just want to see you."

That was it. I could feel the clock ticking down. Something was going to give, and I refused for that to be my family. So, I made the decision to stop pretending that I knew what I was doing simply because it was "working" and we were "successful." I instantly admitted to myself that I needed help understanding how to balance success with happiness.

Coincidentally or by an act of God, I had recently been introduced to Dr. Milu Islam, an accomplished business coach. Everyone in business talks about working "on" your business instead of "in" your business, but the urgency I felt to master this concept caused an unusual amount of nervousness in meeting Dr. Islam. Luckily, we clicked. I knew that this man could help me fill in the pieces missing from my business education; the only problem was I didn't know how I would afford his services. But, after our first session, I realized that time with my husband was worth the coaching fee, which is ironic considering the lesson that became the foundation of changing my life.

What was this life-changing lesson? It was simple—I needed to recognize the most valuable resource on the planet and invest in it. I say simple because that was the easiest part of the journey—identifying the one thing that I needed to leverage to harness success *and* happiness. Learning how to leverage it was the hard part.

Time Bomb

To reach my fabulous potential, I first had to identify the thing that unlocks wealth, both spiritually and tangibly. I didn't have to become Indiana Jones to do it (although I look pretty sassy in a fedora). It's not gold, jewels or artifacts. This secret is limited in supply and finite, but equally available to everyone on the planet. Most would describe it as rare, but when it is harnessed, it has an unlimited rate of return. It's TIME.

Belief Bomb

Next, I had to embrace the concept of Time being the most precious resource on earth. I examined the facts. Each person is given only 24 hours in a day, and those days are diminishing with each sunrise. No matter a person's material wealth, she cannot go to the ATM and withdraw more time than the next person in line.

Now, some may balk at this idea, arguing that 90% of society is trying to claw its way into the wealth experienced by the top 10%; and therefore, the highest value must be attributed to money. But, let's take a closer look at that 10%. Do we really covet their money? Or, are we jealous of the way that they spend their time? They rarely spend a single hour doing something they do not want to do. Cleaning the house? They hire someone to do it. Paying their bills? They hire someone to do it. Working 40 hours a week in their companies? They hire someone to do it. This leaves them free to use their time doing the things they most enjoy. So, our drive to be as successful as those we see on the cover of a magazine does not come from coveting money, but rather from coveting time.

How can we be sure that is the case? By taking a moment and asking ourselves why we are working so hard in our own lives. Take the perspective of the small business owner. Most people that embark on the adventure of owning a business will tell you that they want to 1) do something they love, 2) be able to set their own hours, and 3) earn unlimited income. When we break it down, that dream is about 1) how they spend their time at work, 2) making time for things outside of work, and 3) accessing life experiences that they have dreamed about from behind a corporate desk. It is all about time.

This blew my mind. The majority of my time had been dedicated to work because I was striving to make more money, thinking that was the answer to our dreams. Once I became aware of my misplaced focus on income, I could release the belief that I had to work and work to reach the level of success we desired. I acknowledged that I was in possession of the resource needed to make us happy now. Upon redesigning my beliefs, I was eager to apply this knowledge to a new way of life.

Trust Bomb

The concept of time being more valuable than money is pretty easy to latch onto, but putting it into practice was a little more difficult, and, way outside my comfort zone.

Up until this time, I had operated under the beliefs that "it will be faster if I just do it myself" and "I'm the only one that knows how to do that right." I had trained my employees to complete about 40% of the job duties. Now, my business coach was asking me to hand over another 40% of our operating tasks. Um, didn't he hear me say I'm the only one that knows how to do it right??? Turns out, he knew how to lead me to another revelation.

I had to acknowledge that I trusted my employees and my need to be involved in all aspects of the business flew in opposition to that trust. And, if I trusted them, I would allow them to fail, to learn from their mistakes and grow. Scary proposition. But, once I realized how my actions in the business were limiting and insulting my employees, I became committed.

To let go of the reigns required an intense amount of willpower but was accomplished by reminding myself what was most precious to me – time with my family. So, I ventured outside of my comfy little box and started to feel magic happen by implementing two processes.

Boundaries Bomb

Like most business owners, I didn't have an hourly rate of pay. I knew how much it cost the business to have my employees work X number of hours, but never even considered my own worth to the company. That changed with the Opportunity Cost formula.

On the day my coach introduced me to this illusive concept, it was the first I had heard of it. Since, I have seen it presented in many ways, but this is still my favorite. He asked me two questions: Five years from now, 1) what do you want your income to be, and 2) how many hours a week do you want to be working?

I had big dreams, so I said 1) $5,000,000 and 2) 20 hours a week. We plugged that into the Opportunity Cost formula.

20 hours a week x 52 weeks in a year = 1040 hours/year

$5,000,000/year ÷ 1040 hours/year = $4807/hour

$4807/hour??? Suddenly, that put my individual worth to my company in perspective. Every hour I worked should be contributing to my future income of $5,000,000, meaning, I had to focus on growth activities that would increase our revenue. This made it much easier to identify where I should devote my time. Any task within the business that was not worth $4807 per hour needed to be delegated to someone other than me.

Understanding this concept didn't automatically eliminate my life-long habit of over-working. I had to combine this logic with the reward of execution, so I created boundaries honoring my precious time. First, I removed myself from the operations schedule. I would no longer spend my time on the gym floor. Second, I took a hardline on separating work-time from family-time, ending the work day when my husband arrived home, regardless of being "in the middle of something." Finally, I scheduled a get-away for us once every three months to unplug and focus on each other.

Once I committed myself to this course of action, it took less than three months for me to pull myself out of business operations and concentrate my efforts on growth. It worked. We have since expanded adding two businesses to our portfolio: a travel company and secrtSOS International, a business development company where I teach other owners to make the switch from employee to entrepreneur.

It's ironic. The key to creating my fabulous life was to fearlessly reject my limiting beliefs about success. It feels silly now, but it's a lesson that's easy to digest with a mojito in my hand and my toes in the Mexican sand on our quarterly vacation.

Continued...

April Porter graduated from the prestigious Washington University School of Law and then served the St. Louis community as an Assistant Prosecuting Attorney, specializing in child abuse, sexual assault and homicide cases. Her exemplary record and knowledge of the law led to an appointment as the Municipal Judge for the City of Clarkson Valley. April was a rising star in the legal community when she pivoted to start her first company, Porter Health & Fitness, LLC.

After opening four 9Round® fitness locations in less than three years, April co-founded secrtSOS International, LLC, a business education and development company where business owners learn to grow revenues and scale quickly with a wholistic approach to business. Through this endeavor, she has become a sought-after business consultant and speaker.

April has been published in Yoga and Spa Magazine, featured by Entrepreneur.com and Club Solutions Magazine, and was named one of St. Louis Small Business Monthly's Top 50 Fastest Growing Companies for three consecutive years 2016 – 2018.

april@secrtsos.com
www.secrtsos.com
www.linkedin.com/in/aprilporterbrands
www.facebook.com/9roundwildwood
www.facebook.com/SecrtSOS

VIVIAN SIERRA

Cowgirl Up

I've been a horse lover since way back when. A few years, ago, I was offered and accepted (what was for me) an ideal situation via a connection from my horse trainer. The offer came with access to a beautiful horse farm, my amazing trainer (and human being), acres of trails and a horse to ride. In exchange, the owner of the horse farm had someone she trusted to exercise and care for Luke, her beloved rescue horse. Given that Luke is a rescue, a fearless survivor in his own right, holds particular poignance for this topic! In the end, I got to do what I loved to do, the owner solved her problem, and Luke got exercise. It was a win-win-win. Nothing beats that.

One beautiful day at the ranch, some cowgirls, a cowboy, Luke and I went on a trail ride. On the way back to the barn, as I adjusted my pant leg, I kicked Luke with my spur. His front legs flew off the ground, and I "grabbed leather" as they say in cowgirl speak. Then, to avoid Luke landing on top of me, I let go. I hit the dirt and my head. I got back up on my feet, dusted myself off, and got right back on that saddle. No crying, no whining, no complaining: cowgirl code. These things happen around horses.

After my trainer assured I was okay, he proceeded to share his customary cowboy wisdom. He taught me the importance of how to "cowgirl up" not just with horses, but also with life. He taught me about being fearless.

A lot about riding horses translates into life lessons. You know—good old-fashioned horse sense goes a long way. Honestly, I've been a little short on that, horse sense, but it's never too late to learn. And learn I did, fearlessly! Being around horses, Luke in particular, requires fearlessness, humility and love. So does a life well-lived.

Luke, as does life, requires consistent attention, care, time, discipline and effort—in a word, love. Horsemanship demands humility. Luke is an enormous animal, and he deserves and demands respect. He, as with all horses, relies on his intuition to protect himself from harm. Horses have an uncanny ability to sense emotions and remain alert to any and all things that make them vulnerable. They are honest, real, and indifferent. You can't fake it with a horse; they see right through everyone's (bulls*&t) malarkey. What happened that day, happened. I made a mistake, and Luke responded in kind. He didn't care how I felt. Nor does life. For me, being around Luke reinforced the necessity of integrity in order to live fearlessly and fabulously.

In order to divine how to become fearless and fabulous in midlife and beyond, integrity remains paramount. Fearlessness without integrity is like trying to bake bread without yeast: You, like bread, will not rise.

Getting back on that saddle, rising from the ashes like the phoenix, are familiar themes and experiences for me in my quest for feeling whole. My divorce reignited my sense of independence, my love of horses, and a burning desire to get reconnected to my true self. On the very real side, divorce created new challenges such as single parenting, bankrupting my support system and other uncharted, rough waters. As a result of claiming my independence, I opened a private practice, which I built over 8 years. I went from a whopping $20,000 the first year to $300,000. Then life happened and I had to make the decision to close my practice. I fell, and I fell hard. I felt shame to the core.

After my divorce in 2002, I experienced loneliness. I recall talking to myself, repeating countless times, "I am living in an emotional desert." After closing my business in June of 2013, I ran off to Utah for a year with my tail between my legs, lost. In January of 2014, I drove to Moab with my devoted dog, Lily, by my side. As I was driving, I noticed the beautiful sunset. I pulled over. I had the big "AHA" moment when I found myself still in a desert and still alone. As they say, no matter where you go, there you are. And there I was. That moment gave rise to my blog and the realization that I was working my way back to finding my home within myself. My true self.

All my "mistakes" and "failures" resulted in lessons including getting back up onto Luke's saddle. Yes, I licked a lot of wounds, but I feel fortunate that one stepping stone appeared after the next to get me to where I am today. Am I a picture-perfect vision of the American dream? Maybe not to a lot of people, but how I feel inside about myself and about how I live my life are priceless. Do I have problems and challenges? Yes, of course. But my integrity guides me to make choices and to keep moving forward. As I often tell my clients, you cannot change the fact that problems will arise. The difference lies in your perspective.

In my case, believing that I can grab leather, get back on that horse after I fall, and cowgirl up is THE DIFFERENCE. I made it possible with some know-how, action, a little help from my friends and other welcome visitors in my life. Unexpected events will happen. Learning when and how to grab leather, to cowgirl up, and to get back on that horse have become part of my life's tack box.

Paul Watzlawick, a great thinker about how people change, said, "Perception is not real, but it is real in its consequences." Falling off a horse is likely to happen if you ride horses. It is a risk you must accept. Living life well, perhaps having wealth and/or financial stability, adventure—having a life worth living—comes with taking risks. It goes with the territory.

For me, the life worth living is a life lived with passion, peace of mind and horses! If I have no passion, then I don't feel alive. If I have no peace, then I cannot enjoy life or horses. What I've learned about myself and am willing to say out loud is that I want success. My definition of success? My success as a woman takes fearlessness. Playing it safe; expecting people to do it for me; expecting someone to rescue me—none of this works. I've tried it. I failed. Fearlessness was my buoy. It nudged me to take a good, hard look in the mirror, and tell myself the truth. The truth was that I avoided taking on full responsibility for myself. The truth was that I wanted to be rescued.

My fear was that "I wouldn't and couldn't make it" on my own. I feared pain and loneliness, then fear itself. I became complicit in sabotaging my achievements. My point: Life offers no substitute for making your own way and living on your own terms. I have taken risks, and I have fallen off many a saddle. I have failed to believe in and appreciate or love myself. I have envied others for what they have, or felt ashamed for what I lacked—for not being good enough.

My prize in living fearlessly with integrity lies in living by my rules, my way. Having a healthy indifference as Luke showed me. The rewards are inevitable.

Believing that I can create my own success, that is the difference that makes the difference. Being willing to do what I have to do and whistle while I do it. Being willing to win and to lose. Being willing to saddle up again. To hit the trail again. To grab leather when I have to. Let go when I need to.

Look at Luke. His life as a rescue horse has had trials and tribulations. On any day, he would be willing and able to throw me off that saddle again. He remains true to his nature, which, in part, is to mind his welfare first and stay on the trail. Now, I "cowgirl up" as many times as it takes, knowing that I can do what I have to do and move on—without selling out! My integrity, like Luke's, is not negotiable. Besides my health, my integrity is my most valuable asset.

The desire to be clear about my direction in life and work yields advantageous results. However, make no mistake, my journey to being fearless and fabulous, came at a high and unforeseen price: the loss of relationships. But with the losses have come gains, including far more meaningful relationships, most importantly, with myself.

Being fearless and fabulous has become my new goal. This has opened up doors in many places, including my heart and soul. It bestows a sense of freedom and liberation long unfamiliar to me. Now I allow myself to be vulnerable and to "dare greatly." I haven't completely arrived of course, and God willing, never will. Being fearless and fabulous has taken courage and some blood, sweat and tears; and I wouldn't change a thing.

In order to achieve fearlessness and fabulousness you need to put yourself, your true self, out there. You need to know who you are. If you aren't sure, then you need to find out. Of course, as a therapist, I encourage you to get yourself a fearless and fabulous therapist to help you on this journey. Find a therapist who has done their own work; they should know what you mean by that. Living an integrous life is a work in progress; creating a solid support system is vital. If you don't have a solid support system, don't stress. As a fearless and fabulous aspirant, you will build one along the way; you will attract like-minded people—and possibly horses. Just be on the lookout, and do not settle!

As I said before, integrity lies central to becoming fearless and fabulous. Examine integrity in every aspect of your life. Look at physical, mental, emotional, social, occupational, spiritual and financial integrity. Do not compromise. Integrity depends on remaining focused on the prize, that is, having integrity intact.

In finding your own way back home, remember that home exists within. Adhere to the belief that thoughts create things and believing is seeing. Believe in the benefit of your own hard work, in loving yourself, your body, your mind and spirit, your friends and family, your thoughts, words, and deeds. Love the rewards of your work, in whatever form it comes. As your life goes on, work on doing the next, right thing for yourself, without doing harm to others. Remain focused and steadfast in your goals. However small and humble they may be, they are valuable.

Some days I feel that I have found nirvana; it comes more often now. A bike ride on a sunny day or dancing in the kitchen. Don't expect to find the end of the rainbow. Expect to walk this path made of stepping-stones, one step at a time, with no end in sight. Expect that you will continue to find yourself in circumstances better than you ever imagined. Expect that you will keep the faith, and take things as they come in the best way possible. I expect and hope that you will pay it forward, sharing your fearless and fabulous self, by helping and witnessing countless others have similar and perhaps better life experiences.

Finding your integrity means no more waiting. No more watching. NO more wondering about what's real or not real. Paying more attention to what you know, to your truth, gives you an unending supply of strength. It is your compass. It tells you to be true to yourself. That is the voice of integrity. That is the voice that sets you apart and sets you free. Trust yourself and your process, and you will stay on the path of fearlessness and fabulousness at midlife and forever.

Continued…

Dr. Sierra is a licensed marital and family therapist. She earned her doctorate degree in marital and family therapy from St. Louis University where she was awarded a two-year fellowship from the Graduate School. She also earned an award of distinguished designation from The American Association for Marriage and Family Therapy and the American Counseling Association. She has advanced training in Telehealth/Virtual Sessions, Multicultural Training and Competence, Trauma Therapy and Equine Therapy.

Her career as a therapist and life coach has spanned over 25 years. Prior to that, she worked in hospitals, universities, schools and agencies providing a variety of services including, workshops, public speaking engagements, college professorships, outreach consulting, and a clinical practice. She enjoys working with her clients who continue to teach her about life and the potential of each person and what miracles look like.

Dr. Sierra continues to pursue her mission of "Saving the world one person at a time." Currently, her practice focuses on relationship and individual counseling and coaching. She has a passion for working with women and those from diverse cultures and backgrounds. She has extensive training in clinical psychology, trauma therapy, cognitive behavioral therapy and couples and family therapy. As a therapist and coach, she has helped countless individuals, couples and families improve the quality of their health, relationships and lives.

She invites you to visit her blog, "Working My Way Back Home" and website for additional resources and information designed to better your life.

www.drviviansierra.com/

www.workingmywaybackhome.wordpress.com

www.facebook.com/drviviansierra/?ref=aymt_homepage

www.linkedin.com/in/dr-vivian-sierra-lmft

JULIANN NICHOLS

The End in Mind

I am sitting on the front porch of my 95-year-old house. The sun is about to peak over the horizon and the silence of my St. Petersburg, Florida, neighborhood in the early morning hours is cathartic. I am present in this very moment, just for me. In this beautiful space in time, I realize some things that I wish I could go back and tell my 20-year-old self. In the words that you are about to read, I share a few of these things, with the hope that I can inspire at least one person to embrace the message and take full control of their destiny, now.

For most of my life, I have been "other focused." In my relationships with friends, husbands (yes, there have been more than one), and of course children and family, I, as many of you, have always tended to their needs before mine. I have also put jobs and businesses first. Charitable projects and volunteering FIRST. As women, the majority of us are probably guilty of this behavior.

Have you heard of the "oxygen mask theory"? You know. When the flight attendants tell us, "Put the oxygen mask on yourself first and then help others." So often, we are not putting ourselves first, even though we are well aware that those who practice self-care first tend to others more effectively.

In my early years, I set myself up to focus on caring for others instead of zeroing in on what I needed to do to be a successful individual. I took on and prioritized the role of caretaker.

When I graduated from high school, I went to college on a theater scholarship. I was going to direct movies with Steven Spielberg; yet the decisions I was making in my life were not aligned with achieving this goal. I never even reached out to Steven to tell him that I was coming. I was roaming around making decisions that were leading me away from Steven and my goals. I wasn't focusing with *"the end in mind."* I wasn't focusing on how I was going to reach the pinnacle of my career with Mr. Spielberg. And, I wasn't owning the fact that I was enabling the obstacles that kept me from achieving that dream.

Today, I would look back and write to my 20-year-old self, "Dear Self:: Do you think about where you want to end up? Imagine that you have all of the money you need, what would you be doing? Who would you be with? Where would you be living? Take work out of the realm of possibilities. Volunteer and be philanthropic if you like. But what are you doing for you? Are you travelling the world? Be specific. Where are you going? Are you living on the beach in the winter? in the mountains in the summer? Are you learning how to paint? Spending more time with family and friends? Taking time for YOU? This isn't a when I retire, or when I get out of college, or when the kids leave the house scenario. Think about where you want to be right now."

Now come back to the present. Ask yourself, "Today, what is keeping me from getting where I want to end up?" Most of us would say "money", "time", "clients", "family". Many would say fear of failure, fear of success, fear of lack of knowledge, and so on. I would suggest that you focus on each of your fears for a few minutes. What actions are you or could you be taking to overcome these fears?

We talk a lot about "someday" or "when". Then we don't take actions that will enable that someday to happen. *Why?* It is because we do not navigate our lives with the end in mind. We are not striving for our ultimate goals and what we want our legacies to be. Our fears are holding us back.

So how do we become "fearless"? In reality, it may be impossible to ever become totally fearless. But life has a way of challenging us with our fears. Some of us step up and own them. We try to overcome them. That doesn't mean that the fear goes away. It means that we now respond to that particular fear in a different, more effective way. YAY US! But keep in mind, we do first have to "own it," to identify and admit to the obstacles that keep us from getting to where we want to be.

I started my first business when I was 16, as a mobile DJ in the disco era. That role evolved into radio, college gigs, and nightclubs. During that career I made decisions based on what other people thought. Have you ever had someone say to you, "I think you would be great at____ (insert here). You should do that." Then you go do that to find out that it is not what you wanted to do. And now you're stuck. Why do we "shoulda" people?

When I was 25, I was on my 2nd marriage with two small children. I was working as a paralegal by day and a DJ by night trying to make ends meet. My then husband was not supportive of anything that wasn't financially beneficial. He constantly reminded me that my "end in mind"—working with Steven Spielberg—was just a dream or a "freakin' hobby." "You will never be able to make that happen. Steven is not calling you to direct movies with him."

I worked for a law firm back then. One day, I was forced by my boss to make a choice of either keeping my job or picking up my sick kids from preschool. I quit my job and picked up my kids. When my husband came home, he wanted to know why we were already there. I told him the kids were sick and, "Oh, by the way, I quit my job." All I heard was, "Juliann, what are *you* going to do about that? Call them and get your job back."

Fears of being a failure ran through my head. Thoughts of my kids and my husband soon followed. Then I heard the guy in our law firm who had told me previously that I should be a detective, that I would be good at it. So, I blurted out, "I am going to be a Private Detective." I was shocked that I had said it. My husband's response was, "You will never make it! Stop thinking of yourself and think about this family." It was at that moment, the first time in my life, that I stood up for myself and said, "Watch me."

I started my private detective business, a male-dominated industry, and grew it for 15 years! Maybe I was trying to be good enough for my dad, a former Chief of Police. All I knew was that I wanted to be different and to show that a woman could run an agency right along with the "boys." However, I didn't know what I was doing and worried about what my dad and others would think if they knew.

I am a woman that likes style and bling—and being fabulous. As a kid I would dress up in my finery just to play in the mud. As a grownup in the detective field, my colleagues, called me the "Diva Private Eye," a title worthy of Steven Spielberg. Little did they know that I was afraid to succeed in the business. It sounds counterintuitive but I was trying new things while being in my limitation mindset. I was running my business as if I was an employee. I didn't have a CEO Mindset.

Eventually, I overcame my lack of knowledge, fear of failure/success, and fear of not being good enough. I learned "People don't think what you think". I built a great agency and sold it! Since then I have dabbled in the mortgage business, a handbag business, and during the recession I started a consulting business. Today, I help people shift their thinking to that of being the CEO of YOU!

When you are the CEO of YOU, you make decisions with confidence. You are okay with the outcome. If the decision goes the way you want, you can decide if you need to improve or leave it alone. If it does not go the way you want, you can ask yourself, "What would I do differently?" Then decide, "Should I auto-mate, delegate or eliminate?" We call this A.D.E. Over the years I have learned to embrace each point.

<u>Automation</u> in today's technology age is hard for me. Yet, I have had to embrace it. When I started my first business in the 70's computers were rare and cell phones did not exist. Technology has changed over my 40 year entrepreneur adventure; it has been a challenge to keep up. I am still overcoming my resistance to automation, but learning to use it has freed up a lot of time and angst.

I <u>delegate</u> quite well. I own the fact that there are things I just don't want to do, don't like to do or don't know how to do. I surround myself with people who I can delegate those tasks to. I have a chocolate lab. Her poo is not small and I used to be responsible for picking it up. I don't like to do that. Then, I found out about Poop 911. Yes, there is a service that picks up poo. I delegated it and no longer pick up dog poo. I have built my businesses over the years by surrounding myself with people who have the knowledge, skills and desire to do those things that I do not or cannot do. To delegate is the CEO Mindset.

I have learned to <u>eliminate</u>—most recently, the toxic people in my life. I choose to not be around the people who don't support me. We have eliminated friends and members of our family because of my husband's illness, and I've adjusted to the fact that we do not need them in our lives. I have also learned to eliminate products, services and people that will not get me to where I want to be in my career. The elimination of people and the elements in my life that do not serve me has opened the door to some amazing new relationships and business opportunities.

A.D.E. is an important part of my business and my life. It can be the difference between staying stuck or moving forward. I have come to the realization that I cannot be expected to fix and do everything. When my husband was diagnosed with Dementia and then Stage IV cancer with a 6% chance of making it through a year, my world fell apart. In reality, it was a cleansing and is a true test of my courage and strength. If I weren't in the CEO Mindset, I would be in a corner crying all the time. The end in mind with my husband is to be fully present, to fight right along with him to give him a quality life, and for me to gain more memories with him.

My end in mind has changed over the years. Yours will too. You will find that life will pivot you. You will adjust and make things happen. How you handle these surprises and challenges will determine just how fearless and courageous you are. Know that you are not alone. God did not put us on this earth to handle life all by ourselves. When you keep your end in mind, you will make decisions to get to where you want to be, and you will get there quicker.

My end in mind still has Steven Spielberg calling me to do a movie about the Diva Private Eye. I need to figure out how to make it happen!

Hey, Mr. Spielberg, here I am!

Continued...

A "Serial Entrepreneur" with over 40 years of experience, Juliann Nichols has honed the art of developing successful business strategies. As the owner of a private investigations firm for 15 years, Juliann knew she possessed half of the equation of true success; the other half came when she sold her PI firm and launched a handbag business. In 2008, when recession-weary business owners sought her advice, she launched Focus on You Strategy. For the next ten years, Juliann helped professionals achieve success in their careers and businesses.

Juliann once again closed the doors on a successful endeavor when she closed Focus on You Strategy to pursue a greater vision in JULO Strategy. As CEO, she continues to challenge the status quo and add value to her clients, helping them focus on themselves and shift to a CEO mindset where they achieve the success and fulfillment they seek.

When Juliann isn't strategizing, building careers and businesses, she's pursuing laughter, fun, shoes, Oreos and Malbec, spending valued time with her husband, Bruce, and their chocolate lab, Zoe, as well as visiting with her two adult children and three grandchildren. She loves traveling and visiting family in Kansas.

juliann@julostrategy.com
www.julostrategy.com/
www.linkedin.com/in/juliannnichols
www.linkedin.com/company/julo-strategy
www.facebook.com/JuliannNichols
www.facebook.com/JULOSTRATEGY

A Defining Moment in Time

I often state, "I want to live to be a 100 years old." That means to me a life divided into two halves, Act I and Act II, filled with unlimited supply of wisdom, experiences, and endless learning. Throughout my Act I, I was busy trying to make a living, looking to the future, not living in the present. Now, at the beginning of Act II, I believe that I have found my passion, purpose, and "burning desire." And through presence and gratitude, I have learned to appreciate the flow of life's abundance as it unfolds.

ACT I: Life's path for each and every one of us is so different, so unique, so full of twists, turns and forks in the road. When I was just 20 years old I shared with my parents my "burning desire" to contribute to society as an Entrepreneur. They looked at me and smiled. I thought they heard me and understood me. But my parents and other close family members shared such things as "Why can't you just work a 9 to 5 job and be content", "whose child are you anyway? You're nothing like any of us", "you had a good career as a Legal Assistant."

Why do some pass judgement and see holding multiple jobs as failures? I see my time as a legal assistant and working in various companies as providing golden nuggets of wisdom that have positioned me to be where I am today.

I'm not sure I understood at 20 years old what it meant to be brave, courageous and fearless in fighting the good fight and pursuing my dreams to become an Entrepreneur. At 20 years old, do we really know what lies ahead of us and what career path we wish to take? I know I hadn't contemplated the hard work, perseverance, and can-do attitude that would be required to be an entrepreneur. I do know, though, all these things have helped me find my passion, purpose and "burning desire" to make a difference.

During my Act I, I always heard that Act II would be the very best years of my life. But I struggled to believe this because I experienced so much from ages 20 to 50—opportunities to be a wife, mother, daughter, sister, granddaughter, niece, and friend. I have never taken any of these experiences (good, bad or indifferent) for granted, not even for one minute. I'm grateful for holding down twenty different jobs and/or career roles in Act I that provided business training and development of my strengths. One of the gifts through my first fifty years was the ability of "adaptation"—which means that I tried, and continue to try, lots of things. I took risks in pursuit of my purpose based upon my extroverted personality.

Since March 2012, from the last three years of my Act I to the present, I have embarked on my fearless and fabulous adventure. When I was 20 years old, I thought my parents had understood what I call the "burning desire" in the pit of my belly to make a difference. As I moved into my middle Act I years, my "burning desire" grew to include my then husband and sons; that is, to help provide for the family, to be an exceptional wife and mother, and leave this world better than I found it.

Have you heard the Girl Scout promise "Leave it better than you found it?" Yes, I was a Girl Scout back in the day and, yes, I have carried this promise in my heart every day since. I applied it throughout Act I and still apply it today.

Gary D. Chapman, in his book *The Love Languages Devotional Bible*, wrote, "We receive the gifts of wisdom, insight, experience, expertise, and material possessions to enrich the lives of other people." I believe that enriching each life that I touch with love is leaving the world a better place. I applied this motto and these gifts through my Act I and promised myself back then to continue to do so through Act II.

<u>ACT II</u>: They say "Life BEGINS at 50." I can attest to that because all the same "burning desires" I felt 33 years earlier in ACT I have come rushing in upon my reaching this stage of life. As I move into Act II, yes, midlife—Did I just say midlife?—I reflect back and see that women have come a long way, notably with this word, "midlife." Many of us now have the ability to embrace it, talk about it, and to say it. Try it now! If you are in midlife, say it out loud with me, with no fear. "Midlife!" Whether you are in midlife like I am or you are 20, 30 or 40-something

awaiting this grand period of your life, it is a gift to grow old and impart wisdom on future generations.

I often share with my Mom that some of us get to live out many experiences, gifts and accomplishments in Act I, and then we die. Much like Kobe Bryant, retired NBA basketball player, who died at age 41 before hitting his Act II. While the first fifty years allows many of us to gather life lessons through education, work experiences, and/or hard knocks, the second fifty years allows us to share our collected golden nuggets. I know for certain I am getting to apply my school of hard knocks and life lessons during my second Act II, for which I am grateful.

One characteristic I developed in Act I, and get to sharpen during Act II, is a "NEVER GIVE UP" attitude. I believe that attitude and a positive approach to life are needed daily in order to not lose sight of where we are going and growing yet staying attentive to where we are right now.

Accepting the season we are experiencing, perhaps finding our purpose or "burning desire," takes understanding of the concept of staying present. Through presence and gratitude, we learn to appreciate the flow of life's abundance as it unfolds. We allow the abundance to reveal itself every day that we are given another breath.

Through living love and being present, I've learned to allow others to be who they are and to love them where they are along their paths. I've learned not to change others, control them or cast my opinions on them. I've learned to practice the belief to take what I want of another's good qualities and leave the rest behind.

No two individuals walk life's path in the same way. I speak from experience. Look at the work I do today and for the last seven years. I am an independent bra fitter. There's not many of us out there. I guide women through a bra fitting so they may discover their own personal fearless, fabulous and confident selves through my work. Women drop their walls and learn how a perfect foundation fitting, personalized just for them, makes all the difference in their confidence. I assist them, in a compassionate and supportive way, in order for them to discover their comfortable confidence from inside out. While they may just be learning it, I know that their confidence has been there the whole time, and I get the honor of allowing them to find what is unique to them, through my bra fitting service.

There is a magnitude of reasons that I come to meet my clients. My role helps and supports women both young and old in multiple ways, through multiple seasons of life and multiple physical states of change and well-being. The need for a bra fitter may be related to body image, a disease, or a surgical procedure. I make this often-dreaded experience simple, educational and fun with no inhibitions on their part and no judgement on mine. Many times, I will chuckle together with my client over something embarrassing, while I provide a compassionate and kind listening ear. I communicate with and teach each woman to embrace their body and their own personal style on their own terms. I reassure them that it's okay; I'm there for however long it takes to get it right.

I have been asked by men, "how are you able to talk about bras when you are around me?" My response is, "I guess because I see being a Bra Fitter as the closest profession to providing a medical-related service without a medical degree (I wanted to be a nurse upon graduating from high school).

I owe my ex-husband a great deal of gratitude for insisting I find a side hustle those seven years ago. I looked for work to make the extra money we needed. I fell into bra-fitting; little did I know it would become my passion. I acknowledge my faith and trust in my creator who guides me through purposeful steps. I don't believe in coincidences. I am so very blessed and grateful to have these strong yearnings to be an entrepreneur and of service to women. I get more satisfaction as a provider of this service than my clients do as the receivers.

I believe that my past careers contribute to the career path I follow today. I believe that my life-long desire to be an entrepreneur has affirmed for me, "You are fearless! Don't give up!

Lessons Learned in experiencing Midlife and Beyond…

Believe in yourself, your abilities and your strengths

Nothing or no one can hurt us unless we allow it. Where the struggle comes in is when we try so very hard to seek others approval. We want others to hear and understand us. But finding our individual state of being fearless and fabulous means sharing our authentic vulnerable selves no matter where we are on our journey.

Discover your Fearless & Fabulous Self through your own ACTS I and II

When we are given the opportunity to live two different halves of life and given the opportunity to be active contributors to our families, communities and our world, we are Blessed!! Learning through these blessings yields the discovery of our Fearless and Fabulous selves.

Be grateful! Gratitude is Everything

Like Kobe Bryant, some of us don't get a second chance, an Act II, to expand upon our golden nuggets and let our light shine. It is my prayer that each of us not become content and take every day for granted. Appreciate. Appreciate. Appreciate.

Take a chance or two along the way and find the hero within!

Taking action and/or a chance, taking control and not second guessing or over-thinking every situation, removes a burden off our shoulders. Everything happens for a reason. Always ask yourself what you are meant to learn from the situation.

Along my pathway to this moment, I have discovered some favorite lines that I've come to live by:

Life is what you make it!
You are worth investing in you!

Don't put off till tomorrow what can be done today!
Do it with Passion or Not at All!

I want to live to be a 100 years old. Many think I'm crazy, but I have a lot of sharing, loving, traveling, and experiencing I have only dreamed of doing thus far. Our lives all have meaning and direction if we stay present and watch the daily indicators and occurrences unfold, affirming we are on the right path in the pursuit of our "burning desire." Here in Act II of my life, I live these moments and I believe that I have more defining moments to come!

As a final thought, this story is being written during the Spring of 2020 while we all shelter-in-place. Our faith, trust, patience, and obedience are being tested. As I watch the devastation of this scourge, though, I see the world come together in love for each other. For that I am grateful. This is our fearless "Defining Moment in Time."

Continued…

Michele Petralia is founder and CEO of CeleBRAte Her Style. A bra fitter, foundation consultant and expert based in St. Louis, Missouri, she serves clients across the country.

Michele has been in retail sales for over 10 years as an independent sales representative conducting luxury sales in mid-size to large retail organizations (Nordstrom's, Saks Fifth Avenue, Soma Intimates and most recently Soft Surroundings).

In her current role, Michele is known as "The Bra Woman", "The Bra GuRu for You" or "Stylist for Bodacious Confidence". She answers to all three with pure absolute delight!

Michele has a gift and passion for walking women through bra fittings like none other her clients have ever experienced before. She helps women find the exact size and shape of bra that fits perfectly! Michele is a one-stop resource for all questions relating to bra and undergarment foundations, which provide overall comfort and confidence, which she believes begins underneath the most stylish fashions!

The Bra GuRu for You
CeleBRAteHerStyle.com

www.linkedin.com/in/michele-petralia-b4b17b6/
www.instagram.com/mpetralia/
www.facebook.com/CelebrateHerStyle/
www.twitter.com/michelepetrali1

KAY UHLES

A Wish Your Heart Makes

"♫ A dream is a wish your heart makes / When you're fast asleep...♫"
-Walt Disney's *Cinderella*

I first heard those lines from Disney's *Cinderella* when I was a child. But I did not know how to apply them, nor that they even could be applied to me. Today those words inspire me.

I had fancied the idea of being a writer beginning in my childhood and continuing through my adult years. But many questions—how to start, how to organize, how to form a plot, et cetera—as well as many fears—fear of scrutiny, fear of exposing my inner self, fear of success/failure, et cetera—discouraged my taking on a task such as writing the Great American Novel, or even something less, in spite of many accolades and praises throughout the years.

Upon graduation from high school, my counselor suggested I become a journalist, a writer; however, my family was not college-minded, and I could not imagine a future beyond marrying my high-school sweetheart, starting a family, and being a stay-at-home mom. These were not just my dreams; they were others' expectations of me: "Kay will be married by the time she's eighteen." But they were wrong. We married when we were both twenty. That two-year delay was my first journey into rebellion against others' expectations!

After ten years of marriage and five years of being a stay-at-home mom, I wanted more. I wanted to be a court reporter. As a court reporter, I could write others' words and thoughts. I could sit behind a little black machine, blend into courtrooms and boardrooms, bury my own thoughts from the world, and record dialogue.

Over dinner one night, I explained my desire to be a court reporter, along with my financial how-to plan, to my husband. Afterward, with his conciliatory "That's nice, dear," and his perfunctory pat on the back, I set the plan into motion. I enrolled. Two weeks before I was to begin school, my dream of being a court reporter appeared to crumble before my eyes as I was confronted with divorce.

More fear set in: fear of the kids' and my financial security, fear of the demands of single-parenting—but most of all, fear of having to let go of my dream of becoming a court reporter. Close friends and family (including my soon-to-be-ex-husband) encouraged me to give up the idea of going to school to start anew, doubting that I would—or could—build the speed of a court reporter. They encouraged me to stay in the secretarial position I had held for the last ten years, the position with immediate money and no risk.

Two weeks later, to my ex's dismay, my mother's shock, and a bit of my own surprise, I quit my job and began court reporting school. My next big rebellion against others' expectations!

For four years thereafter, I pounded the tiny keyboard in front of my bay window, while the kids outgrew their pants, their shoes, and my grocery budget. Still, the pounding on the little black machine continued until the ultimate 225 word-per-minute goal was met. Not without blood, sweat, and tears, I had made it. I was a court reporter.

After working as a court reporter for several years, building my own court-reporting business, and having gained a wealth of random knowledge—actuarial, construction, medical, et cetera—I, again, wanted more and enrolled in the local community college.

First class: Composition 101. I was excited to "learn" how to write! At the end of the semester, with the knowledge I had gained from Comp 101, I knew I had returned to my passion. Then came the following semester and the second class: Composition 201. This time it was not without facing my fears at the hands of the instructor. One day during class, she projected an essay at the front of the room. "Let's look at Kay's paper," she instructed the class. "See that. Don't do that." There it was. I shriveled.

Sometime later, after a visit with my Aunt Betty, a writer herself, I called upon enough courage to send one of my stories to her; she shared it with a friend,

"Lou," another writer. Then I received a letter and read it in disbelief: "Lou and I agree: You are a novel-quality writer," my aunt wrote. "You need to write a book." I scoffed, folded the letter, and tucked it away.

After eleven years of college classes, taking one random class at a time (without a plan for graduation, just a thirst for knowledge), I realized that I was on my way to having an associate's degree. Still, I wanted more. I began transitioning out of court reporting and pursuing my undergraduate degree, full time.

Southern Illinois University (SIU) sat just across the Mississippi River from my home in St. Louis. At the age of fifty, I enrolled. After whittling down all my worldly possessions to what would fit into a nine-by-ten room, I moved into a campus apartment with two eighteen-year-old roommates. Strangers. Taking a full load, I spent hours in my room, studying, venturing out into the shared living quarters only to grab a bite to eat and then return.

Among my courses for that first semester was creative writing. About mid-term, my professor invited me to read one of my works at an annual "Reading" with other student writers. I felt honored but fears resurfaced as I read my personal story in front of the gathering. Later that semester, again in disbelief, my professor asked me to join the staff of the department's publication, an anthology of student essays, poems, and short stories. With the goal of learning more about writing, I agreed.

At the end of that spring semester, my roommates moved out. After their move, I enjoyed quiet spring days and evenings on the balcony overlooking the lake, woods, and wildlife. During the summer, again taking a full load, I studied on the balcony, ate on the balcony, read on the balcony, and basked in the sun on the balcony. I even wrote a book on the balcony. Another set of roommates moved into the apartment in August. The 2000 school year was off and running.

The following spring, after two years of being a college coed, I graduated. One day after graduation, I packed up my possessions once more and moved to Colorado to be close to family—and with the intent to write. After I settled in, I unpacked boxes and found the book I had written on SIU's balcony. Two years later, after a tweak here and there, with eyes closed and breath held, twenty-seven book proposals were dropped into the mail addressed to publishers. Within weeks, I received twenty-seven letters of rejection. Again, I turned away from writing in order to make a living as a court reporting teacher.

In 2009, I was introduced to "Mary," who had been told about my writing. Mary invited me to write her memoir and—to my surprise—pay me for it! During several interviews, Mary told stories of personal connections to Frank Lloyd Wright, Walt Disney, and Woody Woodpecker; all of which were told in the backdrop of WWII, Hitler, the Great Depression, and the Hindenburg. Six months after Mary's memoir was privately published—although she and her family had been pleased with the book—spontaneous self-criticism ran rampant through my head. My copy of Mary's bound memoir was put away where no one would find it, to be forgotten. Life went on: grandchildren, a master's degree, a stint at college administration, several personal moves, and retirement. I was lost.

In 2019, I created a writing group at my home. Participants each focused on the retelling of a life story through "Fairy-Tale Diaries." We shared mutual support, brainstorming, and laughter. Lots of laughter! Although the writing group provided a great social release and forum for my writing hobby, all was not fun and games. I struggled to find peace due to a personally tough winter. Many friends embraced me. One friend in particular reminded me that, twenty years earlier when we first met, I had told her I wanted to write. Now she asked, "What have you written lately?" Nothing.

I took those words to heart. Within days, Mary's memoir came out of its ten-year hiding place and into the light. It was dusted off and displayed for others to read. The book which I had written on SIU's balcony was revived and revised after twenty years of dormancy. I found Aunt Betty's letter and a novel began to materialize in my head; its storyboard hangs on my walls today. As a bonus to my writing, I began working as an editor and writing coach. The writers I work with teach and inspire me in so many ways every day! I am grateful for the opportunity to read their fascinating stories, and I look forward to reading many more stories to come.

I have never considered myself fearless; in fact, I have always felt somewhat fearful, as evidenced by my following others' expectations for years. Even after my divorce, I lived by a motto I had often heard repeated by other women: "Living well is the best revenge" (George Herbert, 1640, *Outlandish Proverbs)*. That motto pushed me into doing more in those younger days and succeeding. For that I am grateful. Then I grew up. I learned to lean on intrinsic motivations, my own expectations, and those fabulous words: "personal satisfaction" and "purpose." These words are my rallying cry today.

Have you ever been asked: "If you could have dinner with anyone, dead or alive, who would it be?" My answer has always been Walt Disney. I admire him for his perseverance in the face of some 300 rejections as he sought to get his theme park off the ground. Disney said, "All our dreams can come true if we have the courage to pursue them." Disney, from the beginning, had the courage to pursue his dream to the world's great delight and pleasure. It has taken me decades. *It's a good thing I believe that it is never too late to follow your dream.*

I am a writer!

Consider Walt Disney's words:
"First, think. Second, dream. Third, believe. And finally, dare."

- *First, think:* To paraphrase Dr. Joe Dispenza in a recording of "The Steps to Manifest Your Dreams," (https://www.youtube.com/watch?v=c-mjMA-FsU-M&list=PLIAEuq73Rv4V2665tEc7FQ4CjSx3c8tKV&index=120), think about what you've been thinking about. Become conscious of your thoughts. Thoughts become things. Negative thoughts will become negative things. Yell "Stop!" (silently, of course) until negative voices in your head become still. On the other hand, when someone gives you a compliment, don't scoff or poo-poo it. Accept it! Make it your own belief!

- *Second, dream:* Imagine manifesting the experience you seek—with emotion! Sing it with feeling! Visualize your dream just before going to sleep. Remember… "♫ A dream is a wish your heart makes / When you're fast asleep…♫" Wake up knowing it is done in your life. And be grateful.

- *Third, believe:* Believe in yourself. Believe in the possibilities. Listen to others' positive perceptions of you and believe it! They may know—or accept—more of your innate abilities and fabulous qualities than you.

- *Finally, dare:* Dare to reach for the stars. Dare to be bigger! Greater! Dare to be the fabulous you!!

Continued…

Passionate about personal histories, Kay Clark-Uhles is a writer, editor, writing coach, and facilitator.

As a writer, Kay preserves memoirs, biographies, life stories, ethical wills, and legacies for generations to come. She believes that everyone has a story to tell. It's just a matter of sitting down and writing it—or finding someone to write it for you.

Kay is excited about the release of her first book, *Parts, Pieces, & Particulars: A Primer for Single Moms Raising Boys and Single Dads Raising Girls*, coming later in 2020.

As a writing coach and editor, Kay enjoys assisting new authors in finding and expressing their individual voices. Kay's compassion for each client stems from her educational and MI (motivational interviewing) training experiences.

Kay facilitates virtual and person-to-person "Writing & Wining" groups where life stories, fairy-tale diaries, and other works are created.

Kay graduated from Southern Illinois University with a B.S. in communication and a minor in creative writing, and from Colorado State University with an M.Ed. in adult education and training. When Kay is not creating, she is spending time with family, playing golf, traveling, or watching a sunrise/sunset.

More information about Kay's work can be found at:
KayClarkUhles.com
mindwise.soulworks@gmail.com
https://www.facebook.com/KayClarkUhles
https://www.linkedin.com/in/kay-clark-uhles

The Aura of Change

Beth Wheeler

As she sat on the bluff overlooking the sea to the sunrise,

She felt the wind pick up out of the south and knew change
was in the air.

It nipped at the whisps of her hair, like butterflies flitting gently
around her head.

Her inner voice told her that "this" was the moment all
daydreamers await their whole life.

She sensed before she saw the Phoenix rising.

Its wings of change unfurled their way towards the horizon, then

Reaching for her,

Rolling their way over the water line and up the rippling dunes.

The air was heavy with the Aura of Change.

It enveloped the warmth of the possibilities it brought.

The sun ran pin pricks through her, casting prisms all over her world,
her place where she found and became a woman —
accepting of herself, embracing love and joy.

Her heart's euphoric weightlessness lifted and floated her
onto a cloud.

She had achieved her own life's fairy tale with her own
happily-ever-after ending.

She knew as the sun rose,

Life would never be the same.

She silently thanked Divinity that it wouldn't.

Beth Wheeler is a single mother of two who had the ideal role model in her mom; a woman who was supremely focused on raising her two children. Although family dinners were a mandatory event, they were the highlight of the day. The table was always filled with laughter and love, and Beth continues many of the same traditions her mom instilled in her children—including nightly family dinners.

As the oldest child of divorced parents, Beth picked up both a camera and pen when she was 14, using writing and photography to express her bottled up fears and emotions. Her book *Living with Grace: it's not all puppies and rainbows*, penned under the name of Beth Carsen, is a compilation of her and her daughter's written works and a tasting of her photography. It was borne out of a deep desire to stay connected with her growing daughter while helping her to deal with some of life's ugliness and similar experiences. Together they hope to inspire and assure other females who have faced difficult life experiences: when the darkness feels overwhelming, they are not alone.

Beth Wheeler
Pen Name: Beth Carsen
virginialinepublishing@gmail.com
www.facebook.com/BethSTLPhotography/
www.facebook.com/VirginiaLinePublishing
www.instagram.com/Virginia_Line_Publishing

Made in the USA
Monee, IL
20 May 2020

31073133R00059